RETIREMENT
INCOME
FOR LIFE

SECOND EDITION COMPLETELY REVISED AND UPDATED

RETIREMENT INCOME FOR LIFE

GETTING MORE WITHOUT SAVING MORE

FREDERICK VETTESE

Published by ECW Press
665 Gerrard Street East
Toronto, Ontario, Canada M4M 1Y2
416-694-3348 / info@ecwpress.com

Cover design: David A. Gee
Author photo: Dean Macdonell

Care has been taken to trace ownership of copyright material contained in this book. The author, editor, and publisher welcome any information that enables them to rectify any reference or credit for subsequent editions.

The information presented herein represents the views of the author as of the date of publication. Because market conditions, laws, regulations, and procedures are constantly changing, the examples given are intended to be general guidelines only and the author reserves the right to alter and update his views based on new conditions as they develop. The information and opinions contained herein should not be construed as being official or unofficial policy of any government body or agency.

The material in this publication is provided for information purposes only. This publication is sold with the understanding that none of the author, the editor, or the publisher is hereby rendering specific professional advice. If professional advice or other expert assistance is required, the services of a competent professional should be sought.

LIBRARY AND ARCHIVES CANADA CATALOGUING IN PUBLICATION

Title: Retirement income for life : getting more without saving more / Frederick Vettese.

Names: Vettese, Fred, 1953– author.

Description: Second edition completely revised and updated. Includes bibliographical references and index.

Identifiers: Canadiana (print) 20200289209 | Canadiana (ebook) 20200289225

ISBN 978-1-77041-602-4 (softcover)
ISBN 978-1-77305-642-5 (PDF)
ISBN 978-1-77305-641-8 (EPUB)

Subjects: LCSH: Retirement income—Canada—Planning.
LCSH: Finance, Personal—Canada.

Classification: LCC HG179 .V48 2020 | DDC 332.024/0140971—dc23

The publication of *Retirement Income for Life* is funded in part by the Government of Canada. *Ce livre est financé en partie par le gouvernement du Canada.*

PRINTED AND BOUND IN CANADA

PRINTING: MARQUIS   5   4   3   2   1

To my father, Mario,
whose legacy will live on for decades to come.

TABLE OF CONTENTS

LIST OF FIGURES AND TABLES

PREFACE

Decades ago, a mentor taught me that the urge to edit is stronger than the sex drive. It helps to explain why I felt the need to revise *Retirement Income for Life* a mere two years after its initial release.

In fact, there were many valid reasons to embark on this revision. First, it was necessary to address what turned out to be the most common situation: readers who were still a few years away from retirement wanted to know how they could improve their financial situation in the time they had left. This scenario wasn't explicitly covered in the original book.

Second, I felt inclined to reorganize the chapters into a more logical sequence. We actuaries are nothing if not logical. I also added chapters to address special situations, such as high-net-worth couples, early retirees, single retirees, and early death.

Finally, it was important to reflect some significant developments since the release of the first book. These include the impact of the expanded Canada Pension Plan and the possible introduction of deferred annuities that start at age 85. The biggest development, however, appears to be the fallout from the COVID-19 pandemic. I say "appears to be" since it was still in its early stages as I was completing the manuscript.

In spite of the changes, the five enhancements, which made up the core of the original book, are still intact, although not without some refinements. Ultimately, this new edition is not just a revision; it is more of a reboot, one that I hope will continue to help readers.

FREDERICK VETTESE

APRIL 2020

INTRODUCTION

My first lesson in spending came at the age of four, when I frequently took money out of my mother's purse to buy candy at the local convenience store. (How I got to the store on my own is another story.) Sometimes it would be just a nickel or a dime, but I wouldn't hesitate to grab a five-dollar bill if there was no loose change.

I didn't get away with it, though. My mother or father would get a call from the store saying that little Freddie had come in to buy a five-cent chocolate bar. They would tell the store owner to give me what I wanted and send me home.

My older brother, who was all of six at the time, cautioned that if I kept up my profligate ways, the family would run out of money. There is no evidence that I heeded his warning, which frankly sounded a little alarmist to me even then. Nevertheless, my parents eventually made their money less accessible, which put an end to my shopping expeditions.

I learned two things from this experience: First, it is easier to spend someone else's money than one's own, a privilege I have rarely been able to repeat since age four. Second, I needed a better strategy if I wanted my spending to be sustainable. This book offers such a strategy, though it is geared more for retirees than for four-year-olds.

Drawing down one's savings in retirement is something very few retirees do well, even with the help of professional advisors. Some retirees outlive their money. An even greater number systematically underspend for fear of outliving their money. And many retirees from both camps waste a substantial part of their wealth by employing inefficient drawdown strategies or spending more than necessary on investment fees.

There are several reasons for this sorry state of affairs. First, drawing an income from one's savings was not a mainstream issue until recently. Most of the retirement planning literature to date has focused on the task of *accumulating* money rather than *decumulating* it. Even the latest robo-advisors, which automate investing (more on this in Chapter 27), seem to be more focused on helping people build their nest eggs, not spend them. With over one thousand Canadians turning 65 every day, however, the cultivation of good decumulation practices has become an urgent matter.

Second, it seems nobody wants to see retirees drawing down their savings — certainly not the financial advisor who takes a percentage of their assets each year. Nor do retirees' children, who might fear that they will (a) receive no inheritance or (b) have to support their aged parents in their later years. As for the person who is most aggrieved at seeing wealth diminish — well, it's the retiree. A declining account balance makes one feel financially vulnerable and this becomes an ongoing source of existentialist angst. As I note in Chapter 12, drawing down one's assets in retirement is a stark reminder not only of our dwindling influence in this life but also of our own mortality.

If you have significant savings, I have no doubt that the strategies described here will put you in a stronger position to cope with another financial meltdown such as the one we experienced in 2008, or the one that may be unfolding in 2020. Even if the capital markets behave themselves in the years to come — and let's all hope they do — you can still look forward to more income with less anxiety.

PART I

Identifying the Decumulation Problem

Part I shows that turning a nest egg into a regular stream of income is more difficult than it looks, even when you follow a well-accepted decumulation strategy. A retiring couple called the Thompsons do everything "by the book" and still run out of money. I take them through some basic adjustments to their strategy to get them ready for the enhancements in Part II.

CHAPTER 1

Who Should Read This Book?

Target Audience

Most retirement books focus on the accumulation phase, meaning that they help you to decide how much to save and how to invest as you build your nest egg. In this book, I assume that the reader's accumulation phase is over or nearly over. Rather than salting away more money for retirement, your primary concern is to turn the savings you already have into a steady income stream that will last for the rest of your life.

I am assuming that you have already accumulated significant savings, meaning at least a six-figure amount. For the most part, this money will be held in tax-sheltered vehicles like **RRSPs**, **TFSAs**, and **defined contribution (DC) pension plans**, but some of it could also be stashed away in investment properties, equity in a small business, and bank accounts and stocks that you might be holding outside of any tax-sheltered vehicle.

RRSP stands for Registered Retirement Savings Plan. Contributions made to an RRSP are tax-deductible, and investment income earned is tax-deferred. Income tax is payable only if an amount is withdrawn from an RRSP and taken into income.

Unlike an RRSP, contributions to a Tax-Free Savings Account **(TFSA)** are not tax-deductible. They are nevertheless attractive because the investment income as well as any withdrawals are never subject to income tax.

A **defined contribution (DC) pension plan** is a plan you access through your workplace in which money is put aside for retirement. Contributions are usually made by the employees (you) by payroll deduction and the employer makes matching contributions. The money in a DC Pension Plan earns tax-deferred investment income during the accumulation phase.

While you might have earned some pension benefits in a **defined benefit (DB) pension plan**, I'm assuming that is not the main source of your retirement income. If it were, you wouldn't really need this book.

Defined benefit (DB) pension plans are workplace arrangements that provide a predictable amount of pension income that does not depend on investment results or how long one lives. The lucky participants of DB plans are sheltered from a great deal of risk.

You might have retired five years ago and be wondering whether you are drawing too little or too much from your savings. Alternatively, your retirement might still be a few years off and you want to know (a) what type of lifestyle you'll be able to afford and (b) what changes you need to make in your last few years of work to improve your situation in case you don't like the answer to (a). Finally, you might want to know if you can afford to retire earlier or if you have to push your retirement date back.

Know What You Want

If this book is going to be useful to you, it is important that you truly understand what you want your retirement savings to do for you. This may seem obvious but based on the behaviour of most retirees, what they say they want is different from what they really want.

Retirees say that their biggest concern in retirement — apart from their health — is outliving their money. If that were the case, they would embrace any product or idea that would protect their income while they're still alive without worrying too much about what happens to their money after they die.

That, however, is not how most people act. It is human nature to hate leaving money on the table if one dies early. Imagine putting two options in front of a group of retirees. Under Option 1, the retiree receives less income and might still run out of money at some point but at least he gets to keep most of his money if he dies early. Under Option 2, the retiree receives more income with *less* risk of running out of money but some institution keeps most of his money if he dies early. Guess which option most retirees would choose?

If you really want this book to work for you, you need to commit to the idea that your main objectives are to maximize your retirement income and to ensure it lasts a lifetime.

Takeaways

1. This book is for people who are close to retirement, or who are already retired, and who are going to rely heavily on their own savings to meet their retirement income needs.
2. It is assumed that your primary goal is to maximize your retirement income rather than maximizing the assets you leave behind if you die early.

CHAPTER 2

The Thompsons Are Ready to Retire

Meet the Thompsons

Consider the case of Nick and Susan Thompson. Nick is 65 years old and Susan is 62. Their combined earnings peaked in their final year of work at $120,000, which is just a little above the median for a Canadian household with two breadwinners.

The Thompsons are psychologically ready for retirement as they look forward to being free of the daily grind of the working world. On the other hand, they are a little anxious. Once they cut off their stream of employment income, there is no turning back. They have to hope they can turn their life savings into steady income that meets their needs and lasts the rest of their lives.

The Thompsons are what I will call **mainstream retirees**, the type of people that most readily come to mind when you think of retired people. Mainstream retirees held down a job for most of their working lives, bought a home at some point and paid off the mortgage, raised children and paid their taxes. As Anthony Quinn's titular character declared in *Zorba the Greek*, "Wife, children, house, everything. The full catastrophe."

Almost anyone with a solid employment history and a reasonably good record of saving could be a mainstream retiree: professionals, executives, and successful entrepreneurs, for example. They could also be middle-managers and anyone else who held down a steady job for much of their careers. It is not so much their earnings level that characterizes mainstream retirees as their attitude toward retirement. In particular, they:

- assume personal responsibility for saving enough to finance their own retirement,
- aspire to maintain the same lifestyle that they enjoyed when they were working,
- kept their debt under control, especially in their later working years, and
- won't take too much risk with their investments.

When it comes to planning a bequest (i.e., what they will leave behind for others), they don't have a specific number in mind and, in any event, they won't put that in the way of their decumulation strategy. If they thought about it, they would feel that their loved ones should be happy to inherit the residual value of their estate, which will probably include some financial assets as well as the equity in their home.

On the eve of retirement, the Thompsons have amassed $600,000 in RRSPs. Not bad for a middle-income, two-earner couple and maybe a little above normal for anyone with similar earnings who has been saving regularly for 30 years. Converting this $600,000 into income will form the core of their retirement security. The big question is: how do they do this intelligently?

Saving for retirement isn't always easy and at times you might have wondered if the sacrifice was worth it. Think of the things you had to forgo to make that saving happen, like better vacations, nicer cars, and fancier restaurants.

If your saving days are over, you might think that finally being able to spend your accumulated wealth is the easy part, kind of like scratching a long-endured itch. Unfortunately, that is not the case. Drawing down savings is something very few retirees do well, even when they have the best of intentions.

They Try to Do Everything Right

Even before they mapped out a decumulation strategy, the Thompsons wisely got rid of any debt. They had already paid off the mortgage on their home, as have most people in their 60s. They also made sure to pay off their credit card balance each month and resisted the temptation to take out a home equity line of credit.

If you cannot pay off all your debt by retirement age, I see it as a sign of trouble. It suggests you have been living beyond your means, which will make it just that much harder to rein in your spending after retirement.

Another reason debt is incompatible with retirement is that some of your invested assets will be in bonds or other fixed income assets. These investments will almost certainly be earning less interest than what you would be paying on any debt you owe.

The one argument for not paying off your mortgage before you retire is that you left it too late and the only way you can pay it off now is to withdraw a large sum from your RRSP. I don't recommend doing this since you will almost certainly end up paying more tax than if you made smaller, regular withdrawals over a few years. We will assume that Nick and Susan do not have this problem since they made sure the last mortgage payment happened before they retired.

Their next step is to visit an advisor at their local bank branch. There, they learn that if they want to turn their $600,000 in RRSP assets into regular income, the money should be transferred into a **RRIF** first. Hence, they set up a RRIF account. (If their savings had accumulated in a registered pension plan instead of an RRSP, the monies would be transferred to a **LIF**.)

> **RRIF** (pronounced "riff") stands for Registered Retirement Income Fund. This is the vehicle to which RRSP monies are transferred in order to draw a regular, periodic income. The rollover from an RRSP into a RRIF is tax-free. It usually

happens at the point of retirement but must take place no later than the end of the year in which one turns age 71. Withdrawals are subject to income tax. See Appendix B for more details. If savings had accumulated in a pension plan instead, the monies would be transferred to a LIF instead.

 LIF (pronounced "liff") stands for Life Income Fund. It is much like a RRIF, but with a few extra restrictions. See Appendix B for more.

They also talk to family, friends, and other people who seem to be knowledgeable about investments. Their aim is to identify the most prudent and commonly accepted strategy for drawing down their savings.

After much research, here is a summary of what Nick and Susan decide to do:

- invest their RRIF assets in well-known mutual funds;
- draw an income equal to 4 percent of their RRIF assets in the first year of retirement;
- increase that drawdown in future years at the same rate as inflation;
- avoid annuities, which everyone agrees are nerdy at the best of times and especially unattractive in the current low-interest environment; and
- start their **CPP** and **OAS** pensions immediately upon retirement — in this case, at age 65 for Nick and at age 62 for Susan — to extract the greatest value from government pension sources just in case either of them dies early.

An **(immediate life) annuity** is a contract in which you give an insurance company a lump sum (like $100,000), which is called a single premium. In return, they pay you a fixed monthly or semi-annual amount for the rest of your life.

> **CPP** means the Canada Pension Plan (or its Quebec counterpart, the QPP) and **OAS** means Old Age Security pension.

Let's get one thing out of the way before going any further. I could keep on using the term "drawdown," but I prefer the term **decumulation** instead. It suggests a certain symmetry because it is the opposite of "accumulation," which is what you were doing all those years you were saving for retirement.

> **Decumulation** is the process of drawing down one's financial assets after retirement with the primary goal of producing a regular income, usually for the rest of one's life.

The decumulation strategy described above is known as the 4-percent rule. Notice you do not draw down 4 percent of assets every year under this rule, just in the first year. In future years, the amount withdrawn increases with inflation.

The mutual funds that the Thompsons choose, by the way, are from a big-name investment company with a reasonably good track record. They put 50 percent in **equity funds** and the other 50 percent in a fixed income (bond) fund. The annual fee is 180 **basis points**, which is by no means low, nor is it especially high in the world of actively managed retail mutual funds. Because the fees are quietly deducted from their portfolio, paying them is relatively painless.

> Consider **equities** to be another word for stocks. Owning the stock of a given company essentially gives you a share in the ownership of that company. When you put your money into an **equity fund**, you essentially hold shares in many different companies. Such diversification lessens your risk, but you will still experience gains or losses over any given period.

A **basis point** is 1/100th of one percentage point, so 100 basis points equals one percent. If the annual investment management fee on a $100,000 investment is 200 basis points, you pay $2,000 a year.

When the Thompsons describe their decumulation strategy to their friends, everyone nods in approval. Every aspect of the strategy adheres to best practices. It would seem that long-term financial security is all but assured.

Assuming the Thompsons achieve median investment returns in every future year, Figure 2.1 shows what they could expect in terms of future income from all sources, assuming they encounter no nasty financial surprises.

Figure 2.1. What the Thompsons are hoping for

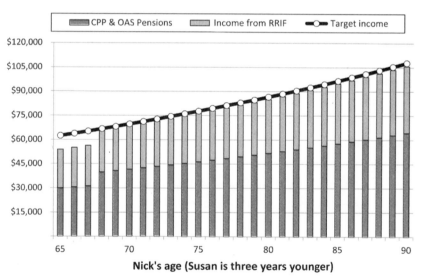

Nick's age (Susan is three years younger)

The Thompsons hoped for median returns. Note the income gap in the first 3 years before Susan starts to receive OAS.

Even this rather rosy scenario is less than perfect since the couple's income is lower in the first three years than it is in later years. This is because the 4-percent rule implicitly assumes that all other sources of income are going to be smooth and steady for life; i.e., no jumps or dips ever. This is not true for the Thompsons, since Susan's OAS pension doesn't start for three years yet. And it certainly isn't true in general, since it is very common for retirees to have other sources of income that are not smooth or permanent. Consider for example:

- rent from an investment property that they will eventually sell,
- part-time employment for a few years after they retire from their regular job, and
- a possible inheritance down the road.

In the case of the Thompsons, drawing less income until Susan starts to receive her OAS pension produces an outcome that is precisely the opposite of what they really want: to splurge a little in their early retirement years to celebrate their new freedom. If there is ever a time to spend more money, it is while one still has the energy and enthusiasm to try new things. We will be fixing this problem in Chapter 5.

In spite of these qualms, the Thompsons would be pretty happy if Figure 2.1 truly represented their financial future. Unfortunately for the Thompsons, what actually happens is nothing short of disaster. This is described in the next chapter.

Takeaway

1. A conventional decumulation strategy sounds like a prudent course to follow, but it can lead to disaster.

CHAPTER 3

The Thompsons Face Financial Ruin

The Thompsons had hoped to achieve a median return on their investments. When one invests in risky assets, though, even such a modest goal is far from guaranteed. In the case of the Thompsons, the capital markets do not co-operate.

As it happens, the Thompsons end up retiring precisely when the long bull market for stocks has finally run its course. Stocks fall sharply from all-time highs and then languish in the doldrums for a prolonged period. This is similar to what happened in the 1970s in North America. It occurred again in the United States in the 2000s, a period known as the lost decade for purposes of investing. Japan has been mired in this state since the early 1990s.

Even the fixed income part of their portfolio (which they invested in a bond fund) does not do too well. That is because interest rates in this nightmare scenario inch up from their ultra-low levels over a period of several years. While that sounds like a good thing, rising interest rates create capital losses on longer-term bonds.

They Suffer Spending Shocks

To compound their misery, the Thompsons incurred some unexpected expenses. Five years into retirement, they had to replace their roof. They did their best to cut back on other spending to make up for it but still ended up drawing $20,000 more income that year than they had planned.

Three years later, their son, Brett, ran into financial trouble of his own. He had bought his first house but then lost his job and couldn't make ends meet for a few months. Like the good parents they are, Nick and Susan stepped in to help. They dipped into their RRIF to give Brett $20,000 and cut back on their own spending by $4,000 in that year.

And finally, at age 78, Nick had a surgical procedure that restricted his activities for six months. The out-of-pocket expenses that Nick and Susan incurred, including hiring caregivers for a few months, set them back another $25,000. Once again, they cut back on other discretionary spending (like travel) while Nick was recovering so their net over-spending that year was $18,000.

Figure 3.1. Actual result: the Thompsons outlive their savings

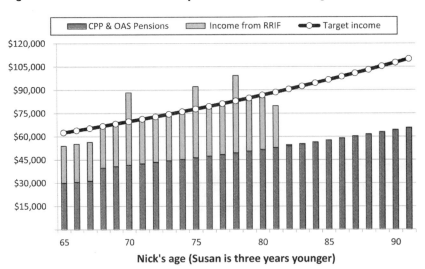

The Thompsons suffer worst-case investment returns. The spikes in income at 70, 75 and 78 reflect higher withdrawals to cover spending shocks. RRIF income runs dry by the time Nick is 81.

In spite of the investment losses and the unexpected expenses, Nick and Susan gamely stuck to the 4-percent rule and increased their income from the RRIF by the rate of inflation. As Figure 3.1 shows, the result was not pretty. They exhaust their RRIF assets by the time Nick is 81 and Susan is 78, which is a real problem since they could very well live another 15 years.

Could This Result Have Been Avoided?

Clearly, doing everything "by the book" does not guarantee a positive outcome as real life has a way of offering up nasty surprises. This is certainly true in the case of spending shocks, which are hard to avoid, but you could prepare yourself for them a little better and be ready (at least financially) when they occur. This is the subject of the next chapter.

Even more problematic than the spending shocks was the use of the 4-percent rule to determine income each year. As we will learn in Chapters 5 and 6, better solutions are out there.

On the question of investment risk, it is fair to ask whether the Thompsons took on too much risk by putting half their money in stocks after retirement. I will save this issue for Chapters 7 and 8.

Ultimately, I will show that the Thompsons could have started out with the same $600,000 in assets, encountered the same spending shocks and poor investment returns, and still enjoyed a comfortable standard of living for the rest of their lives.

Takeaways

1. Decumulation is not as straightforward as it seems; disaster can strike even if you save a lot and follow a widely accepted decumulation strategy.
2. The 4-percent rule doesn't work when investment returns are very poor.

CHAPTER 4

Coping with Spending Shocks

As we saw in the last chapter, the Thompsons encountered three spending shocks after retirement. They cut back a little on other spending to offset the impact, but the shocks nevertheless made an already difficult situation even worse. Below, we help them come up with a better method of handling spending shocks.

In general, a spending shock is any significant expenditure that you could not reasonably predict and cannot ignore once it happens. Hence, refinishing your basement after it has flooded would be a spending shock, while renovating that same basement just because you feel like it falls under regular spending.

Not every expenditure is so black and white. For instance, if your grown-up children continue to live at home after you retire, you might consider the higher bills for groceries and utilities to be a spending shock. On the other hand, perhaps you anticipated this unhappy event and gradually built it into your budget. In that case, it is just another item in your regular spending basket.

To inject a little (actuarial) science into the matter of spending shocks, I will turn to a study that was conducted by the Society of Actuaries (SOA) in 2015. In the study, the SOA enumerated the various different types of spending shocks encountered by Americans and how they actually cope with them.[1] I will focus on the middle-income survey respondents.

The 2015 study was not the first time the SOA surveyed retirees and pre-retirees, but it was the first time the SOA focused specifically on older retirees. The real-life experiences of people who have been retired for 10 or 15 years provide useful insights that cannot be gleaned from theory.

Types of Spending Shocks

The SOA report listed the various financial shocks that retirees reported. When I looked at the list, the shocks seemed to fall into two major categories. The first category consists of supply shocks in the sense that they all involve a sudden loss of assets and the belt-tightening actions that must follow from such a loss. Using the wording from the report, supply shocks include:

- a drop in home value of 25 percent or more,
- running out of assets,
- a loss in the total value of savings of 10 percent or more due to poor investment decisions or a bad investment,
- bankruptcy,
- a loss in assets due to victimization by a fraud or scam, and
- loss of a home through foreclosure.

Notice that the supply shocks all relate to investment risk in some way. I will look at investment risk separately, in the next chapter.

By contrast, the spending shocks all required a sudden, unavoidable increase in spending. Table 4.1 shows the list of spending shocks compiled by the SOA. The table also shows what percentage of retirees experience these shocks according to the SOA's findings.

Table 4.1. Spending shocks in retirement

Shock	Frequency
Major home repairs or upgrades	35%
Major dental expenses	26%
Significant out-of-pocket medical or prescription expenses	8%
A family emergency	6%
Significant damage to the home due to a fire or natural disaster	2%
Divorce during retirement	2%

In reviewing Table 4.1, three observations come to mind. First and foremost, the financial impact is not that large for the most part. Consider major home repairs, for example. These repairs could include things like re-shingling the roof or replacing the furnace, which could cost as much as $20,000 but, more often that not, will be just a fraction of that. While a $20,000 bill is distressing, it doesn't arise that often. With a little bit of planning, this is something that retired couples like the Thompsons should be able to handle.

Home *upgrades*, as opposed to repairs, can cost a lot more, but they are less frightening than repairs for the simple reason that you can opt not to make them. In my own definition of shocks, I didn't include the expense of an upgrade because you can see it coming and you can change your mind about it if you think you can't afford it. It's not as if you walked into your kitchen one morning and discovered workers setting up scaffolding.

Hence, the second observation is that many of the events on the list are not even shocks in the true sense of the word. Even most home repairs should not come as shocks. Roofs and furnaces last only so long and homeowners should not be surprised when they eventually have to be replaced. The oxymoron "foreseeable shock" comes to mind.

Moving on to major dental work, the cost is once again going to be in the low thousands. This might cause you to delay or cancel some discretionary spending — like your next holiday — but it is not going to bankrupt a well-heeled retired couple.

As for medical situations, the chances that the cost will be catastrophic are exceedingly slim in Canada because our universal health care system covers most of the big-ticket items. One study shows that healthcare expenditures of Canadian households at the 90th percentile are about $4,000 a year.[2] This means that nine times out of ten, such expenditures will be less than $4,000. Now, $4,000 is an inconvenience, but it is not going to lead to financial ruin for a couple that is otherwise well prepared for retirement. Besides, you have to assume that anyone who is spending this much on healthcare will be curtailing other activities, so total spending should rise by less than the cost of the healthcare expenditures.

One of the few truly expensive healthcare expenditures that might not be covered are certain new drugs that can cost $1,000 a month or more. There is some real exposure here, though fortunately the need does not arise very often.

If the retiree insists on going out of the country for medical treatment (especially to the United States), then yes, the bills can quickly lead to financial ruin. This is a matter over which the individual has control, however, and it is seldom done voluntarily except by the especially affluent. If medical treatment is needed while travelling out of country, well, there is no excuse for not having out-of-country emergency medical insurance.

Then there is the matter of significant damage to, or loss of, a home. The emotional shock is real, of course, and some items of sentimental value can be lost, but it should not result in significant financial loss; this is what home insurance is for.

My third observation is that the biggest spending shocks are ones that tend to involve other family members. Divorce after retirement is one of those events. It is not so much the legal costs that set you back, but rather the fact that your assets drop by half while your living expenses drop by only 30 percent or so. I confess I have no solution for this unfortunate eventuality other than to oversave if you feel it is a real risk.

The crises of other family members can also cost you money. One common situation will be a grown-up child coming to you with an urgent need for money — due to business loss or job loss, for example — and needing financial help. If you feel it is your role to be your adult children's financial backstop well into your retirement when your own resources are limited, it is not my place to tell you differently. Just be prepared to deal with the consequences. I know of retirees who have taken out sizeable mortgages on their homes to bail out a child, even though they have no way of repaying the amount.

Ability to Cope

You might think I am being a little cavalier in brushing off the impact of the various spending shocks, but the retirees in the SOA survey will back me up on this. When asked about their ability to manage within new constraints (following a shock), 93 percent of the retirees in the top third of the income scale said they managed "very well" or "somewhat well." Based on their assets, Nick and Susan would comfortably be in this top third. So would most of the target audience for this book. As for the middle third of retirees, 85 percent said they managed "very well" or "somewhat well."

What we are witnessing here is a widespread phenomenon that is not usually appreciated by pre-retirees or retirement experts who are opining on the needs of retirees. Retirees are amazingly resilient in difficult financial circumstances. They have a great capacity to "get by" when their income suddenly drops or when they encounter a spending shock.

My guess is that if the same survey was conducted in Canada, an even higher percentage of retirees would say they were managing very well. Not only are Canadians better savers and more prudent spenders (at least that is my impression), we have the **Guaranteed Income Supplement (GIS)** as a backstop. In addition, our so-called socialized medicine is much less likely to result in a major bill to the patient.

> **Guaranteed Income Supplement (GIS)** is a monthly non-taxable income benefit that is provided to Canadians with limited means after age 65. The amount payable is income-tested. If you and your spouse are receiving OAS pension, the GIS cuts out when income is above $24,576 (2020 level).

Conclusion: Set up a Reserve

What do we do with this information? It appears that most retirees muddle through reasonably well, in spite of the odd retirement shock. They do so even without an elaborate strategy for dealing with spending shocks. They should do even better if they approach the matter a little more scientifically. I suggest that retirees like the Thompsons should set aside somewhere between 3 percent and 5 percent of their spendable income each year, specifically to deal with spending shocks.

This reserve might not totally cover all the shocks that people like the Thompsons might encounter, but it will definitely soften their impact. It would certainly place the Thompsons among the better-prepared retirees. I should add that this is a strategy best suited for middle-income retirees. Those who qualify as "high net worth" should rarely have a problem covering their spending shocks.

If you do set up a reserve, I would strongly suggest using the money only for rainy-day situations. To avoid the temptation of treating it as mad money, you might want to keep it separate from other assets. In the original scenario, Nick and Susan didn't build a reserve to handle spending shocks. In the makeover, we will assume they set aside 3 percent of their retirement income until age 75 (a little under $2,000 a year, plus inflation). This may not turn out to be enough, but it will at least mitigate the pain of any spending shocks they encounter.

The idea of holding a reserve also helps to explain a mystery. I used to think it strange that retirees would bother saving any money at all and stranger yet that so many of them save as much as they do. They were originally saving for retirement, but now they are retired, what is all that saving for? It appears that many retirees sort of back into the idea of holding a reserve against future spending shocks, whether they know it or not.

Long-Term Care Situations

The SOA survey did not consider long-term care as a spending shock. Long-term care is a complicated issue that deserves more space than there is room for here.* Let me say, though, that it tends to be a real financial problem for only a small fraction of the population. Most people will never need long-term care, and many of those who do will need it only for a relatively short period of time, like one or two years.

As for the rest, the very affluent can handle the extraordinary costs as they arise. Those of modest means will have to rely on family members and community care access centres in any event. It is only the people in the middle-income group who need to make some hard decisions. Those with substantial equity in their homes might choose a more expensive option, such as home care with outside caregivers.

Takeaways

1. Most spending shocks that you are likely to encounter in retirement are modest enough to be manageable.
2. The biggest spending shocks tend to be events involving family members, like divorce or extending financial support to a grown-up child.
3. Contribute 3 to 5 percent of your income to a reserve fund until age 75 or so, and use this reserve to cover spending shocks.

---

* I addressed it at some length in my book *The Essential Retirement Guide: A Contrarian's Perspective*. But that is hardly the final word on the subject.

CHAPTER 5

Improving on the 4-Percent Rule

The Thompsons used the 4-percent rule to set their initial income target. That means they drew $24,000 in the first year of retirement from their RRIF. In subsequent years, they increased the amount they were drawing from the RRIF by inflation. In addition, they received pension income from OAS and CPP.

Given that they ran their nest egg down to zero when Susan was still in her 70s, the 4-percent rule is obviously less than perfect. We have already identified one problem with it: it doesn't produce a smooth stream of total income when other sources of income aren't smooth.

There is a more fundamental problem with it, though, which has to do with increasing the payouts each year by the rate of inflation. You might wonder, What's wrong with having your retirement income rising with inflation? If you really need that much more income each year, nothing is wrong with it. But if you naturally start to spend less after a certain age, then drawing that extra income is increasing the chances you will eventually go broke.

As it turns out, most retirees eventually spend less in real terms once they reach a certain age. This is true whether they have a little money or a lot. Once they reach that point, the drop in their real spending from one year to the next may be small, but it makes a significant difference over time.

There are two reasons why most older retirees spend progressively less. First, the particular basket of goods and services that they consume is constantly changing with age. By the time you reach age 80, the contents of that basket will bear little resemblance to what it was when you were 60, much less 40. It would have been sheer coincidence if their real spending didn't change as well.

The other reason they eventually spend less is that they consume less over time. What is amazing is that this finding should come as a surprise to anyone. I sort of knew about this phenomenon when I was 20. I received cash gifts every so often from my grandmother even though she had only a modest income (a small government pension from Italy). As it happens, her spending needs were even more modest.

I'm not the only one who knew something was going on, of course. In his 1977 book on the state of retirement in Canada, Geoffrey Calvert observed that "as age advances, clothing and footwear expenditures fall steadily to less than one half . . . furniture costs fall to one-third . . . automobile-related costs to one-sixth, while travel costs as a whole drop to less than one-quarter."[3]

Calvert went on to say, "Even though the incomes recorded in this sample become significantly less as age advances, the ability to make gifts, add to assets and purchase discretionary and luxury items, seems to be surprisingly well sustained. One does not see reflected here a picture of increasing hardship as age advances."

If Calvert's remarks were true in 1977, they should carry even more weight today. Since the 1970s, Canada's seniors have grown steadily more affluent. Calvert's observations, however, have been all but forgotten. Most of us still think that our retirement income needs to keep up with inflation.

Just because we choose to ignore a phenomenon doesn't mean it no longer exists. The data still suggest that older people spend less. It is hard otherwise to fathom how they could be saving such large amounts. (Yes, older Canadians save a greater percentage of their income than younger Canadians.) According to a CIBC study, the elderly in Canada will be handing over a mind-blowing $750 billion to the next generation over the next ten years alone![4]

If we fail to acknowledge the true spending patterns of older retirees, political correctness may have something to do with it. The mere suggestion that older people don't need quite as much money can come across as senior-bashing. But while it is a sensitive subject, I don't think that justifies our shying away from the truth. By perpetuating myths, we would be doing a disservice to the retirees themselves, as well as to those planning for their retirement. If new retirees know what's in store for them, they can recalibrate their spending intentions early on to reflect that reality. In other words, they can spend more now, knowing they will be spending less (in real terms) later on. This should make them feel less anxious about their future financial prospects.

I mentioned to a friend a while back that older people spend less, and he immediately objected. He said his widowed dad (who was in his mid-80s) spent all kinds of money. I said, "Really? On what, may I ask?" He opened his mouth to answer me but stopped himself. He suddenly realized that most of his dad's extra spending was not on himself but on others. For instance, his dad was paying the rent for one of his adult daughters. What he spent on himself had shrunk down to practically nothing as he seldom went out and no longer travelled in his later retirement years.

Academic Studies on Retirement Spending

If there is any lingering doubt that seniors start spending less in **real** terms, then numerous academic studies from a variety of countries should dispel it. These studies, based on extensive data, make a compelling case that the drop in spending at older ages is a widespread phenomenon in developed countries. The tipping point for the slowdown in spending seems to occur in one's early 70s and then persists well into one's 80s.

> **Real** spending refers to the level of spending after it has been adjusted for inflation. If inflation and spending both rise by 2 percent a year, one would say that real spending remains constant.

Here are some of the key findings from those studies:

- In 1992, Axel Börsch-Supan studied the saving and consumption patterns of the "very old" (his words, not mine) in Germany.[5] By observing 40,000 households, he found that retirees tended to maintain their spending in real terms during their 60s. This result was expected. What surprised him was what happened around age 70. Instead of retirees continuing to draw down their savings, their assets started to *climb* again. Börsch-Supan determined that this happened because older German retirees spent less in real terms. Eighty-year-olds were saving more than 45-year-olds! After testing all the possible reasons for the decline in spending, he concluded that the reduced spending stemmed from two causes. The first was a reduced ability to spend due to creeping infirmity. If you can no longer get on a plane, your travelling expenses decline. The other cause was a diminished inclination to spend. After the death of a loved one, for instance, exotic travel might seem less enticing.

- Actuary Malcolm Hamilton produced a landmark study in 2001 that showed that seniors in Canada save enormous amounts of money.[6] Senior couples aged 75 and over either saved or gave away as cash gifts an average of 16.1 percent of their income. Couples age 85 and older saved or gave away even more. Saving so much indicated that super-seniors must be spending less. More important, it also showed that the drop in spending had little to do with insufficient income.

- The only plausible conclusion is that the elderly are either not inclined or not able to spend as much as they used to. Hamilton's finding is especially compelling given that the study encompassed seniors at all income levels, not just the wealthy. The average income for couples 85 and over, for instance, was just $31,300. While Hamilton used data from the late 1990s, his findings should be just as valid today given that modern-day seniors are much better off. Incomes among seniors have risen nearly 20 percent in real terms since the mid-1990s.

- David Domeij and Magnus Johannesson reported that Swedes also spend less as they age. Their 2006 study tried to explain why.[7] The explanation that best fit the data was that failing health made spending both more difficult and less enjoyable — essentially the same conclusion as Börsch-Supan's.
- A 2015 UK study (Brancati et al.) sifted through two very large data sets: the Living Costs and Food Survey, and the English Longitudinal Study of Ageing.[8] They uncovered a precipitous drop in spending between ages 60 and 80. In spite of it, most of the 80-year-old respondents said that their spending was not constrained by a lack of money. The reductions in spending occurred at all income levels, by the way. Similar to the Börsch-Supan work, the tipping point for a slowdown in spending occurred around ages 70 to 74. As the authors noted, this is also when time spent at home alone starts to rise rapidly.

You might be wondering why I have not cited any Canadian studies other than Malcolm Hamilton's, which is now more than 20 years old. It is because good Canadian studies are hard to find. One possible reason for this, as mentioned earlier, is political correctness, a force from which even academics are not immune. A more tangible reason is that **longitudinal data** on consumption does not exist yet in Canada.

> **Longitudinal data** refers to data gathered from observing the same subjects over a long period of time.

McKinsey & Company Canada did their best to overcome this deficiency using data from Statistics Canada's Survey of Household Spending.[9] They showed that spending drops sharply with age. Not everyone accepts this finding, however, as it was not based on longitudinal data and was not corrected for changes in household size. These apparent shortcomings do not mean the McKinsey findings were wrong; it's just that longitudinal data would be so much more compelling.

There is one recent Canadian study that suggests that the inflation rate for seniors is in fact a little higher than for younger Canadians.[10] That study, however, speaks only to the basket of goods and says nothing about the gradual change in consumption. A longitudinal study of actual retirees would have been more useful.

For now, we have to rely heavily on the results from Germany, Sweden, and the UK. The studies from these countries are hard to ignore. The data we do have for Canada makes it hard to argue that Canadians are fundamentally different.

Here are some metrics that help to pinpoint how fast spending declines:

- A 2012 Employee Benefit Research Institute study by Michael Hurd and Susann Rohwedder concluded that real (inflation-adjusted) spending by college-educated married couples fell by 1.23 percent a year in their late 60s, 1.75 percent a year in their 70s, and 2.75 percent a year in their early 80s.[*]
- Another study from the United States, this one by David Blanchett of Morningstar, estimated that real spending declined by about 1 percent a year in the first ten years of retirement, 2 percent a year in the next ten years, and 1 percent a year thereafter.
- A third US study, produced by J.P. Morgan using its own data, found that real spending among affluent households dropped by 1 percent a year for the first 20 years of retirement.
- The 2006 Swedish study mentioned above calculated that consumption fell by 25 percent between ages 60 and 80.
- The UK (Brancati) study reported that a household headed by an 80-year-old spends 43 percent less on average than a household headed by a 50-year-old. If one includes mortgage payments in the calculation, then 80-year-olds spend 56 percent less. The researchers used this and similar data to estimate that household expenditure in retirement fell by

---

[*] The Employee Benefit Research Institute (EBRI) is a Washington-based think tank.

1.4 percent a year. This is after having adjusted for various factors such as household size.

Incidentally, all the above studies (except for the McKinsey study) made adjustments to reflect changes in household size over time. The usual reasons that households get smaller are because of children leaving the family home or the death of a spouse.

When it comes to the impact of household size, by the way, there is a broad consensus in academic circles that spending in a household is proportional to the square root of the number of persons in the household. Hence, the living expenses for a single retiree are about 70 percent of the expenses for two (one divided by the square root of two). The death of a spouse should therefore result in a reduction in household spending of about 30 percent.

Setting an Income Target for Future Years

Taking all the foregoing studies into account, I believe it is reasonable to conclude that the spending of most seniors in real terms keeps up with inflation until age 70 or so, and after that it will usually fall at the rate of:

- 1 percent a year throughout one's 70s,
- 2 percent a year in one's 80s,* and
- 0 percent from age 90 and on.

When we factor these percentages into the retirement income target, we get the result depicted in Figure 5.1.

In the case of a couple, this series of reductions begs the question of what happens if the ages of spouses fall in different decades; for instance, what if one spouse is in his 70s and the other is in her 60s? I confess I'm not exactly sure of the answer myself, so I have erred on the side of caution. I have assumed the reduction in spending in a given year is the smaller of

---

* Note that these percentages are slightly different from those used in my book *The Essential Retirement Guide*. This reflects increased conservatism and the inclusion of data from a wider set of studies.

Figure 5.1. How the income target should change

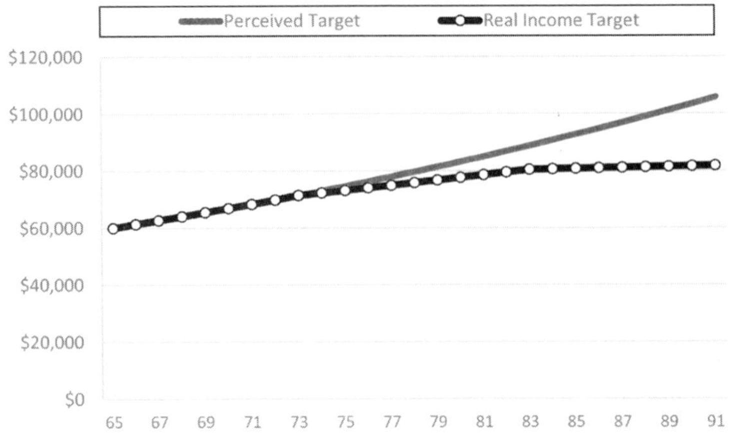

The income target should rise as shown by the black line, not the green line. This chart assumes inflation of 2.2% a year.

the two. For instance, when Nick is 82 and Susan is 79, I have assumed that real spending declines by just 1 percent rather than 2 percent. And as mentioned above, there would also be a one-time reduction in spending of 30 percent when a spouse dies (not illustrated here).

We will now apply this to Nick and Susan. We will build in everything we've learned in the last two chapters. In particular:

- The 4-percent rule showed significantly lower income for the Thompsons in the first three years of retirement. This was because Susan's OAS pension hadn't started yet. We will eliminate this shortfall by having the couple draw enough extra income in the first three years to fill the gap.
- We will assume the same three spending shocks but will show that the bumps in extra income needed in those years have now been either eliminated or at least reduced by the creation of a reserve.
- The new income target curve will be used.

We still haven't established whether the starting income amount is sustainable, but let's assume for the time being that it is the right amount.

Figure 5.2. Add a reserve and reset the income target

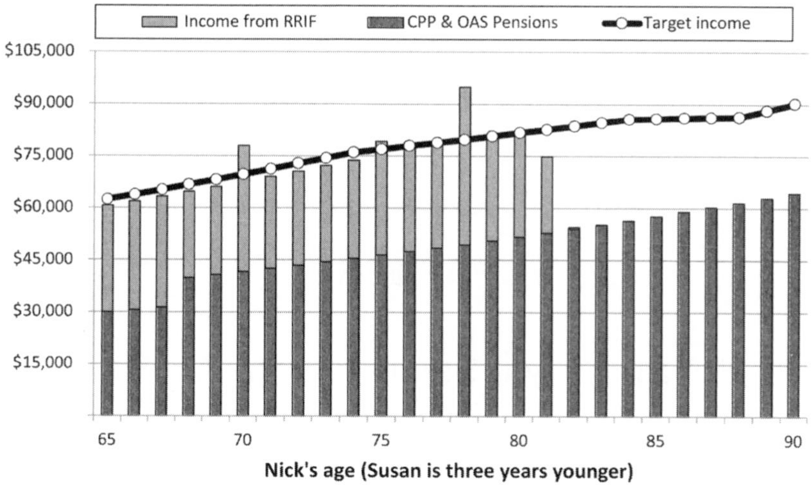

The income gap in the first three years has been filled in and the reserve fund has softened the impact of the spending shocks. RRIF and TFSA income still run out, however, by age 82.

(More on this later.) The result of these modifications is shown in Figure 5.2. The Thompsons are still running out of money way too soon, but this will be rectified later on.

Takeaway

1. Spending by retirees tends to rise more slowly than inflation, especially between ages 70 and 90. This is true even if they have the financial means to spend more.

CHAPTER 6

Withdrawal Strategies to Avoid

The previous chapter illustrated how your income needs change over time. You might be tempted to ignore all that theory and use one of two very popular strategies to determine how much income you will draw each year. In this chapter, we will show why neither one of them is very good.

Withdrawing a Flat Percentage

Some retirees find that withdrawing an ever-increasing percentage of their assets each year is a frightening prospect. They would prefer to draw an annual income equal to a flat percentage of their assets instead. For instance, it might be 5 percent or 6 percent of their RRIF account balance as of the start of each year. Drawing a flat percentage is easy to understand, and it ensures you never run out of money.

The obvious problem with a flat percentage is that it runs afoul of the RRIF rules regarding minimum withdrawals (described later in this chapter). If you choose 5 percent, for example, you will be offside by age 71 when the minimum RRIF withdrawal percentage is 5.28 percent (and rising). Choose 6 percent and you are offside by age 77.

You can work around this technical problem by taking a portion of the monies that you are required to withdraw from the RRIF each year and redepositing it into a TFSA or a bank account. Note that the unspent amount cannot go back into the RRIF, and if you have no employment income, it can't go into an RRSP either. Since the money was withdrawn from a RRIF (or LIF), you are required to pay income tax on it. As a result, there may not be as much to redeposit as you would like.

The real problem with a flat percentage withdrawal is that the income pattern it produces does not reflect your actual needs. This can be seen in Figure 6.1, where we assume that 6 percent of total assets is withdrawn from savings each year. If Nick and Susan achieve 5th-percentile investment returns, their income starts above the income target but then falls below it within three years, even though they still have $150,000 left in their account at age 92. While the simplicity of withdrawing a flat percentage is appealing, it is not a good long-term decumulation strategy.

Figure 6.1. Drawing a flat 6 percent each year

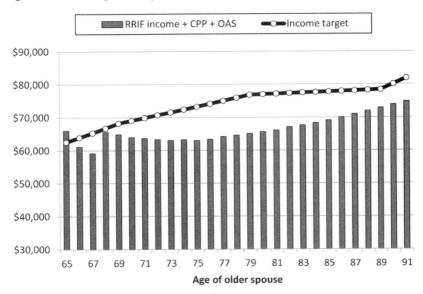

This shows annual income equal to 6% of the RRIF plus CPP plus OAS. It assumes 5th-percentile returns. It produces income well below the income target in most years even though $150,000 in assets remain at age 92.

Withdrawing Only the Interest

According to one professional survey, only two people in ten intend to spend down their assets in retirement.[1] The rest of the retired population try to live off the growth on their investments, or even hope to continue growing their assets after retirement. Apparently, most people really hate to touch their principal.

A decumulation strategy in which one spends only the investment income might be suitable for people who have minimal assets and are ready to limit spending to what their CPP and OAS pensions can buy. They cannot afford to part with their modest capital because they might need it to deal with a spending shock.

Spending only the investment income might also make some sense for the lucky retirees with six-figure investment income. The investment income alone might give them all the lifestyle they want, and it might be a source of great comfort knowing that the intact principal can be used to meet any spending shock or perhaps be used after their death by their loved ones.

For middle-income people like Nick and Susan, however, an interest-only strategy makes little sense. Figure 6.2 shows why. It uses actual investment returns and inflation from 1952 to 1986 to show just how volatile investment income can be. I used this period because inflation and interest rates were low at the start of it, so it bears some resemblance to the current economic environment. In some years they will have much more income than their target and in other years much less. In years where there is a net investment loss, I got around the RRIF minimum withdrawal rules by assuming the withdrawn amounts would be set aside rather than being spent.

I suppose Nick and Susan could have improved on this decumulation strategy by banking the excess return in good years (i.e., ages 67, 71, and 74), but that would have increased the unspent amount at the end of their lives. I can somewhat understand the popularity of this strategy. It is a crude form of risk management for people who don't know what they don't know (meaning most of us), but the result is too far from the ideal income pattern shown earlier.

Figure 6.2. Withdrawing only the investment return

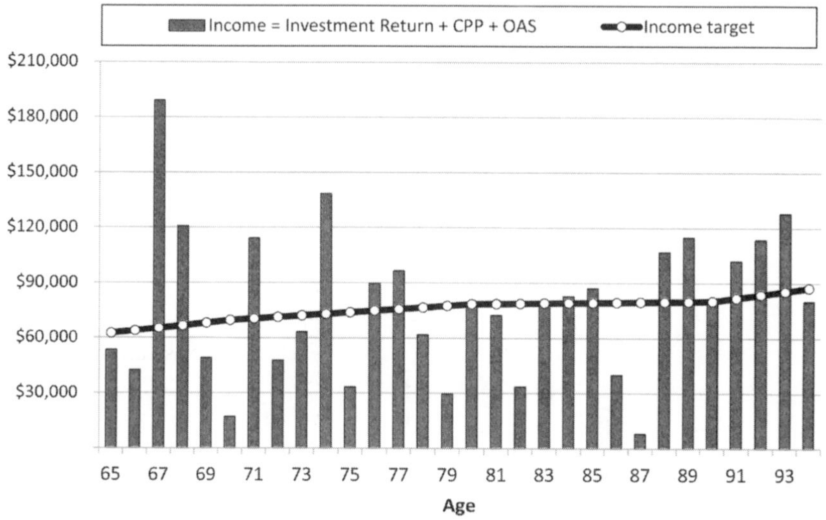

The annual amount withdrawn is the total income, including capital gains and losses. The returns and inflation rates were taken from the 1952-1986 period to simulate real-life conditions.

Making the Minimum Permitted Withdrawal

Under the simplest decumulation strategy, you do what the government says you must do with tax-sheltered savings. Income tax regulations specify the minimum percentage of your total assets that you *must* withdraw each year if your money is in a RRIF or a LIF. The minimum at age 65 is 4 percent. It rises in steps to 5 percent at age 70, 6.82 percent at 80, and 11.92 percent at 90. The minimum finally plateaus at age 95 at 20 percent. You do have the option to withdraw more in any year, but you cannot withdraw less. Details on the minimum and maximum limits are given in Appendix B.

Of course, withdrawing more than you need does not mean you have to spend it all. You could choose to spend less and redeposit the rest, say to a TFSA. This possibility was mentioned earlier, as was the problem that there would be a little "shrinkage" due to income tax being payable on the withdrawn amounts.

Withdrawing the minimum amount each year produces a surprisingly good pattern of income. In the case of median investment returns, the income that Nick and Susan receive is close to their ideal income pattern. This is shown in Figure 6.3.

Figure 6.3. Making the minimum RRIF withdrawal

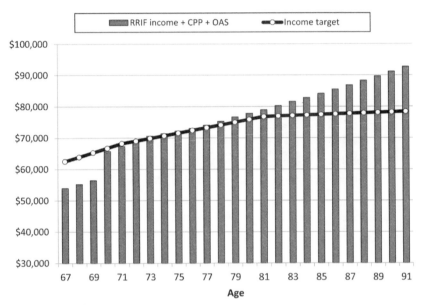

Making the minimum RRIF withdrawals (plus CPP + OAS) tracks the income target fairly well, assuming median investment returns.

This RRIF minimum withdrawal strategy looks better in theory than it does in practice. Here, we are assuming that returns are fairly stable but we know that actual returns on a portfolio of stocks and bonds can fluctuate wildly from one year to the next.

We should be happy that RRIF-based withdrawals work as well as they do, and certainly this decumulation strategy works better than the 4-percent rule if investment returns are suboptimal. Nevertheless, the preferred solution is to draw income based on the ideal income pattern described in Chapter 5.

Takeaways

1. Investment losses will happen every so often; a good decumulation strategy should be able to absorb them.
2. Withdrawing the same percentage of assets each year does not work well. In general, you need to withdraw an increasing percentage of your assets with age.
3. Most retirees want to leave the principal amount of their nest egg intact, but this strategy makes sense only at the extremes of wealth.
4. Withdrawing the minimum amount permitted under the RRIF rules is not a bad decumulation strategy, but you can do better.

CHAPTER 7

Investment Risk

So far, I have described two of the reasons the Thompsons ran out of money — incurring spending shocks and using the 4-percent rule. But let's face it: none of this would have mattered much if they had earned decent returns on their investments. Instead, their returns were much worse than average and stayed that way throughout their retirement years. This raises two important questions:

1. Just how bad was it?
2. Is it better to avoid risk altogether?

Just How Bad Was It?

The Thompsons chose to invest 50 percent of their retirement assets in equities (stocks) and 50 percent in fixed income (bonds). The 50 percent in stocks is assumed to be invested in the **S&P/TSX** Capped Composite Index and the **MSCI** World Index. To be clear, this was not the source of their problems, but we will nevertheless take a closer look at their asset mix later in this chapter.

> **S&P/TSX** is an index that tracks the performance of Canada's biggest companies that are listed on the Toronto Stock Exchange.
>
> **MSCI** stands for Morgan Stanley Capital International. The MSCI World Index tracks the performance of over 1,600 companies around the world.

Equity investments have good years and bad years, as do fixed income investments, but in the case of the Thompsons, I assumed that their returns were generally bad year after year. To put it into technical terms, I assumed their overall returns were at the 5th percentile, year in and year out. This means the returns they achieved were better than only 5 percent of all possible outcomes, no matter how many years we are looking into the future.

You may be wondering why I didn't assume returns closer to historical norms. When it comes to retirement planning, I believe it is wiser to hope for the best but to plan for the worst, and a 5th-percentile scenario is not out of the question. By definition, there is one chance in 20 of realizing a 5th-percentile result.

Percentiles and Monte Carlo Simulations

The brief explanation above of what it means to have 5th-percentile returns may not paint much of a picture, so let me use an analogy. Imagine you want to know how much rainfall Toronto is likely to have next June. It so happens the average rainfall for that month is 89.9 millimetres based on historical records. An average, however, isn't very descriptive. What are the chances it will rain 150 millimetres in June or less than 30 millimetres?

You would get a better idea of what to expect if you had access to historical records showing June rainfall in each past year. Just to keep things simple, we will retrieve just 20 years of data. The result is shown in Figure 7.1.

You can glean some tidbits of information from Figure 7.1 that you can't get from just knowing the average. For instance, we now know that the amount of rainfall can vary widely, from as little as 26 millimetres (2016) to as much as 191 millimetres (2010).

We can make this annual data even more useful if we organize it from the least rainfall to the most rainfall, as in Figure 7.2. We no longer bother to show the year underneath each bar since they are no longer sequential. Think of each year as a "trial" with 20 trials in all.

Figure 7.1. Actual rainfall in June 2000–2019 (Toronto)

Figure 7.2. June rainfall sorted from least to most

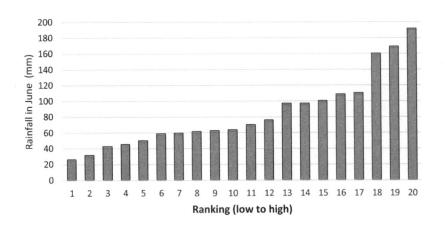

If this 20-year sample was statistically significant (it's not), then Figure 7.2 tells us there is just one chance in 20 that the amount of rain will be 26.4 millimetres or less. Rounding up, we will consider 27 millimetres to be the 5th percentile. The 95th percentile is about 170 millimetres. The median (the point where half the trials are more and half are less) is between 64 and 70 millimetres, so let's call it 67 millimetres.

Now, if I threw out the low and high results in the rain data, I'm left with the range from the 5th percentile to the 95th percentile. This is represented by the solid green bar in Figure 7.3 with the black horizontal line being the median.

Figure 7.3. Range for June rainfall in Toronto (5th to 95th percentile)

You'll note this chart is much more compact than the previous one. Even though it no longer depicts each trial, it still manages to capture the most useful information. For instance, we now know there is a 50 percent chance of more than 67 millimetres of rainfall in June. We also know that there is almost certain to be between 26 millimetres and 191 millimetres. Even though a result outside this range (which would be above or below the bar) is possible, it is unlikely enough that we would ignore it for most decision-making purposes.

This is essentially how a Monte Carlo simulation of investment returns works, but with two differences. First, one needs closer to 2,000 trials rather than 20 to be confident enough that we have really determined the range of possible results and the median. The second difference is that a Monte Carlo simulation for investment returns doesn't use historical data, or at least not directly. Each trial is based on historically observed behaviour, but it is still an artificial trial, a simulation if you will, one that is produced by using a random number generator.

Running Monte Carlo simulations is a sophisticated mathematical process, and I'm grateful to the Morneau Shepell actuarial team for running the Monte Carlo simulation used in this book.

The analogy to Toronto's rainfall will help us to understand the limitations of a simulation of investment results. When we established the 5th percentile, the 95th percentile, and the median for rainfall in June, we made the implicit assumption that the last 20 years was a typical period and that the future would be no different than the past. In fact, it could be different in ways we cannot yet quantify — consider the impact of climate change, for example.

Similarly, future investment returns could be different from the past, with a greater or lesser range of results and a higher or lower median. Just like factors such as climate change could make future rainfall patterns different from the past, a factor such as an aging population or diminishing natural resources could change the investment climate, which could in turn affect interest rates for a long time to come.

With these disclaimers in mind, Figure 7.4 shows the range of likely investment returns for a portfolio that is invested 50 percent in stocks and

Figure 7.4. Range of returns for a 50-50 asset mix

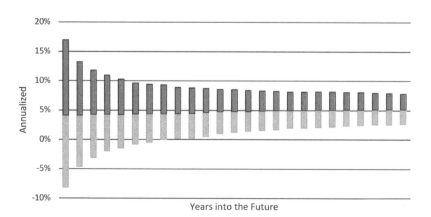

50 percent in bonds. Each of the bars contains information about the range of returns in much the same way as the bar for rainfall did in Figure 7.3.

The bottom of each bar shows the 5th-percentile **annualized returns**. These are the returns, before deducting investment fees, that Nick and Susan are assumed to earn each year in retirement. I am calling this the worst-case scenario, which is a slight misnomer since it doesn't show the bottom 5 percent of scenarios. The top of each bar is the 95th-percentile return. We can ignore the 95th-percentile scenario or anything better than it for planning purposes since (a) it is unlikely and (b) it would be good news if it happened, not something we either should be or need to be planning for. The junction between the dark green and light green is the median return.

Take a moment to study Figure 7.4, as it captures almost everything we need to know about the risk and opportunity associated with a 50-50 asset mix. For example, the annualized 5th-percentile return is negative until year 9. The median return doesn't break above the 5 percent level until year 18, and after that it stays there for all future years. As for the 95th-percentile scenario, the annualized return after 25 years is slightly under 8 percent. All figures are before deducting investment fees.

Annualized return, over a given period, is the average annual return that if compounded produces the same result as the actual returns over that period. For instance, if actual returns are 2 percent in year 1 and 10 percent in year 2, the annualized return for the two-year period is 5.92 percent.

Here are a few observations based on the chart:

- Even under the worst-case scenario, you should expect positive returns if you invest for a long-enough period. The trouble is that much of your retirement nest egg could be gone by the time the market reverses direction in your favour.
- The gap between the annualized returns under the best-case and the worst-case scenarios narrows over time, but the

gap between the outcomes grows ever larger thanks to the magic of compound interest.

- The median return is surprisingly low. In the long run, it is expected to be just a shade over 5 percent, and it will be even less after deducting investment fees.

The last point bears emphasizing. A long-term median return in the 5 percent range is a far cry from the 8.6 percent median return that pension fund managers earned between 1960 and 2015. There are several reasons why future stock market returns will be lower than we are used to seeing. One is that inflation will probably be closer to 2 percent rather than the average of nearly 4 percent that has prevailed since 1960. Another is that pension fund managers invest about 60 percent in equities rather than 50 percent. A third reason is that the bond portion of portfolios will not do as well in the future because interest rates are so low. Long-term bonds can achieve high returns when interest rates go from high to low (as they have done since the 1980s) because they are producing capital gains as well as regular interest. For this reason, it is practically impossible to obtain high returns on bonds when the starting point is low interest rates.

Is It Better to Avoid Risk?

If poor investment performance was the main reason why the Thompsons ran out of money, it suggests that risk-averse retirees would be better to shun stocks and long-term bonds and invest their money in something safer, like **T-bills** or **GICs**.

> **T-bills** is short for Treasury bills. These are short-term investments issued by national governments, including the Government of Canada, to regulate the money supply and to raise funds on the open market. They are offered with terms of 91, 182, and 364 days.

> **GIC** stands for guaranteed investment certificate. It is an investment that offers a fixed, guaranteed return over a fixed period such as 1, 3 or 5 years.

To any investment manager, such an idea would seem outlandish and even border on heresy. After all, risky investments have always outperformed safe investments by a wide margin over the long term. A dollar invested in T-bills at the beginning of 1934 would have grown to $37 by the end of 2018. While that may not sound too bad, a dollar invested in long-term Canada bonds over the same period would have grown to $153. As for Canadian stocks, the same one dollar would have soared to $2898!

On the other hand, the investment horizon of a retiree is not all that that long. If they follow my advice in later chapters and spend down their savings in their early years in return for higher government pensions in their later years, their investment horizon could be as little as ten years. Sustained losses, or at least dismal returns, over this length of period are certainly possible. Besides, the reward for taking risk will likely shrink in the future, if Figure 7.4 is any guide. At a minimum, you owe it to yourself to investigate what would happen if the entire nest egg were invested safely, with no chance of a loss of capital.

To test this scenario, I used the interest rate currently offered* by a Big-5 bank for savings accounts, in which the money is locked in for one year. Such an investment is about as safe as it gets. There is a possibility that interest rates will drop further but it doesn't seem too outlandish to assume the Thompsons will be able to earn 2 percent in a savings account year in and year out. Figure 7.5 shows what the result would be.

This outcome should give one pause. Instead of running out of money by age 82, which is what happened when they invested in stocks and bonds, the Thompsons now have steady income that continues to grow into their 90s. They can sleep at night knowing they are practically immune from a market crash.

In a rare flash of prescience, I first published an article describing this strategy in *The Globe and Mail* in January 2020. At the time, the idea seemed

---

*   As of March 2020. This will no doubt vary over time.

Figure 7.5. The Thompsons put their money in a savings account

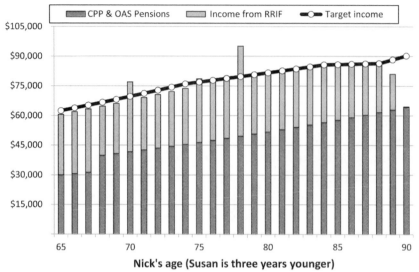

This is the same as Figure 5.2 except the fund now enjoys a 2% annual return in a savings account. The RRIF income now continues to age 89.

questionable at best, since the median return on balanced funds in 2019 was 15.78 percent,* and stocks had generally done well for over the past decade. Then the bear market of 2020 started in early March. Articles started to surface of how people who were getting ready to retire could no longer afford to do so.

The Thompsons do pay a price for all that peace of mind, though. They are giving up the chance to do better. In fact, it is more than just a chance; once the 2020 bear market bottoms out, it is *likely* they will fare better than the worst-case scenario I have been showing. Nevertheless, I know some risk-averse retirees who would and probably should choose the no-risk alternative if they truly understood the implications of each option.

I should point out that this alternative wouldn't be too attractive if interest rates on savings accounts fall to 1 percent or lower. Until a few years ago, this wouldn't have seemed possible, but neither would seeing long-term bond yields below 1 percent!

---

* From Morneau Shepell's *Performance Universe of Pension Managers' Pooled Funds*.

In Part II, we will find that there are ways to enhance retirement income whether the Thompsons decide to take investment risk or not.

Alternatives to Stocks

If you don't want to invest in stocks but do want higher returns than what a savings account offers, what options do you have? A popular alternative these days is real estate. Some people buy one or more condo units and rent them out. This can be profitable when the local housing market is doing well, but disparities from one region to another can be wide, and even robust housing markets do not rise in a straight line forever. Condo investors can lose everything if they hold mortgages on their rental properties, have trouble finding a tenant, and the real estate market cools. The consequences are especially painful if interest rates rise at the same time. This is what happened to many people when the Toronto and Vancouver housing bubbles burst in 1989, and there is no reason it can't happen again.

Real estate might still produce good returns in the future, but you face a host of problems. The first is liquidity. It can take many months to sell a condo, and you cannot afford to be illiquid if a spending shock arises and you need the money to make ends meet.

A second problem is finding a suitable investment property if you have only a smallish amount to invest. In the real estate market, even a few hundred thousand dollars is considered small potatoes.

Third, transaction costs like commissions and land transfer taxes can be considerable and will cut into any capital gain you might hope to realize when you eventually sell.

Finally, don't underestimate the potential hassles of managing a rental property. You need to maintain the property, find the right tenant, and collect enough rent to make a decent return after property taxes and maintenance costs.

All in all, real estate investing is not for amateurs. My advice is to steer clear of this investment class after you retire (apart from your own home) and stick with stocks for capital gains.

Alternatives to Government Bonds

Almost everyone who invests in bonds does so by buying units in a bond fund rather than holding individual securities. Bonds have traditionally been considered a safe investment, or at least safe compared to stocks, but the Monte Carlo simulations run by Morneau Shepell suggest they will be almost as risky as stocks in the future. Bonds do well when interest rates are high and going lower, but they do badly when interest rates are low and rising. Right now, interest rates are at the lowest they have ever been, lower even than in the Great Depression. If they rise, it will create capital losses that will offset the return from the interest that bonds are currently paying. And if interest rates don't rise, your return on bonds will consist only of the interest they pay, which isn't much.

As an alternative to investing in a bond fund, some people lend out money in private transactions in the form of a second mortgage. They do this to get the extra yield compared to bank deposits, but this practice can be quite dangerous. I know of people who have tried it and lost their capital when the borrower couldn't make the payments.

Instead of a plain vanilla bond fund, you might want to consider a fund that consists of **high-yield bonds**. High-yield bonds are always corporate bonds rather than government bonds. They are riskier than regular government-issued bonds since there is a much higher chance of default or at least a downgrade in the bond rating, which usually happens at the worst possible time: when the markets are tanking. A downgrade would precipitate a significant drop in the value of the bond. Ideally, you want an investment that isn't so closely correlated to stocks. When stock markets do especially badly, however, high-yield bonds tend to follow suit. You might put a smallish portion of your overall portfolio in a high-yield bond fund, but I wouldn't bet the farm.

At the other end of the risk spectrum, you could stay completely liquid and invest only in government T-bills. This strategy is safe but doesn't provide much of a return. At the present time, the interest rate on T-bills is even lower than in a savings account in which your money is locked in for a year. In fact, the interest rate on T-bills is lower than the current inflation rate (which is about 2 percent) so your investments in T-bills would be slowly losing value in real terms.

T-bill interest rates may eventually rise but don't count on it. An aging population puts heavy downward pressure on interest rates. In summary, investing heavily in T-bills makes sense only if you have decided to go the super-safe route (see Figure 7.5) and the interest rate you are getting on T-bills is higher than what the banks are paying on savings accounts. Otherwise, consider having only a smallish percentage of your money in T-bills, for the sake of liquidity.

Long-Term Government Bonds

If you're a new retiree, it is too bad for you that this isn't 1982. Over the 37-year period from 1982 to 2018, Government of Canada bonds achieved an annualized return of 7.07 percent a year *after* inflation. This was better than the return on stocks over the same period.

Unfortunately, the stellar performance that bonds achieved cannot be repeated. They were great investments when interest rates were high and trending downward, but it appears that interest rates are about to bottom out, if they haven't already done so. The 1950s used to be considered a period of exceptionally low interest rates, with long-term government bonds yielding about 3 percent. Now, they yield well under 2 percent. In fact, at the time of writing, bond yields have fallen below 1 percent for the first time ever.

They could go a tiny bit lower, but the more likely scenario in the next few years is for rates to inch upward a little. It may be counterintuitive, but rising interest rates create losses, not gains, if you are holding long-term bonds. For these reasons, traditional long-term government bonds will not be a great investment.

Instead, you might consider real return bonds. These are also long-term bonds issued by the Government of Canada. What makes them different from regular bonds is that they promise to pay you interest at a rate that at least keeps up with inflation, no matter how high inflation might go. Another advantage is that real return bonds can be bought and sold easily. They do, however, have one very serious drawback these days. The real yield on these bonds has fallen very close to 0 percent, a far cry from the 1990s, when the real yield exceeded 4 percent. A low yield is a problem in itself but that is compounded by the fact that you would suffer a capital loss if real interest rates were to rise after you bought the bonds. I have already explained that this is a distinct possibility for **nominal** yields; that is also true for real yields. As a result, the case for real return bonds in your portfolio has never been weaker than it is now.

> A **nominal** return ignores the effects of inflation. Most people who are not actuaries or investment experts think in nominal terms. The real return is the nominal return less inflation. For instance, a nominal return of 5 percent when inflation is 2 percent means the real return is 3 percent.

In conclusion, the best hope for decent returns in the years to come — by which I mean a return of 5 percent a year, not 8 percent — is to invest in stocks, risky as they are. If you have exceptionally low risk tolerance, you might want to revisit the no-risk savings account option described above.

Exchange-Traded Funds

To the extent you invest in either stocks or fixed income securities of any type, I strongly suggest that you participate in a pooled fund, such as a mutual fund or an index that one can buy in the form of an **exchange-traded fund (ETF)**. I strongly urge you not to become a stock-picker or day trader or to buy some highflier on the tip of a friend. The odds are very much against you. Even a broker's stock recommendations are unlikely to turn out better than random picking.

> An **exchange-traded fund (ETF)** is an investment product that you can buy or sell in the open markets just like a stock or bond. It is more complex than a typical stock or bond, though, since it owns a basket of assets and divides

> the ownership of that basket among the investors. Unlike traditional mutual funds, ETF fees are much lower since they strip away layers of fees such as trailer fees and sales charges.

I used to research the market on my own and trade in individual stocks. It was hubris to think I was smarter than the crowd and could profit on a consistent basis by taking a contrarian stance. Over time, I did pick a few winners, but I also picked way too many losers. I didn't beat the market anywhere near often enough to call the experience a success. Today, I invest only in the pooled funds of an institutional manager. I picked an investment manager who is part of a major bank, because they are not apt to "go rogue" on me. There are enough risks out there that cannot be avoided; the least you can do is to steer clear of risks that are totally avoidable.

60-40 vs. 50-50

So far, I have been assuming that the Thompsons invest their RRIF monies 50 percent in stocks and 50 percent in bonds (a 50-50 mix). This is what most people do when they reach retirement age. It is more conservative than 60-40, stocks to bonds, which is what professional pension fund managers have seen fit to maintain for decades. The greater conservatism seemed appropriate, as retirees are more risk-averse than the sponsors of large pension plans. On the other hand, we have just seen that long-term bonds and other fixed income investments don't appear to be too attractive for the foreseeable future. So maybe 50-50 isn't better than 60-40 after all?

If we rerun the Monte Carlo simulation using a 60-40 asset mix, the result is a little surprising. Under the worst-case scenario, the Thompsons run out of money at virtually the same time as they did under the 50-50 scenario. In other words, the 5th-percentile return is no worse under a 60-40 mix than it is under 50-50. This is telling us that bonds will be just about as risky as stocks in this current low-interest environment.

Let's take this analysis a step further and see what would happen if the Thompsons enjoyed median investment returns in all years instead of 5th-percentile returns.* We find that with either asset mix, the Thompsons now have enough money to meet their income target in all years, but the 60-40 mix is better. As is shown in Table 7.1, the amount of assets left over at age 92 more than doubles by switching to the 60-40 mix.

Table 7.1. Situation with median investment returns

	Remaining assets at age 92
With a 50-50 mix	$91,000
With a 60-40 mix	$196,000

The advantage of the 60-40 mix versus 50-50 grows even larger if one achieves investment returns at the 95th percentile. Table 7.2 summarizes these results.

Table 7.2. How a 60-40 mix compares to 50-50

With 5th-percentile returns	60-40 and 50-50 about the same
With median returns	60-40 is better
With 95th-percentile returns	60-40 is much better

Given these findings, I would recommend a 60-40 asset mix over 50-50 in the case of a recently retired couple, provided they have some tolerance for risk. Unless indicated otherwise, please note that all the case studies shown for the remainder of this book are based on a 60-40 mix.

I concede that in two rather unlikely situations, a 50-50 mix might be preferable. In the first instance, it would be true if bond yields go even lower, although there isn't much room for this to happen. The Monte Carlo simulation I used to assess the different asset mixes assumed that

---

* We are still assuming they draw $62,500 of income in year 1, with increases for inflation in later years.

bond yields will rise slowly in the next few years, and while that is the more likely scenario, it is not a certainty.

The other instance in which a 50-50 mix might be better is if you encounter investment returns even worse than the so-called worst-case scenario I have been using so far. We will delve into this grim prospect in the next chapter.

Takeaways

1. Future investment returns will almost certainly be lower than historical returns for many years to come.
2. You might be able to avoid 5th-percentile investment returns by putting all your money in a savings account.
3. Stay away from investing in second mortgages.
4. Real estate investing can be lucrative for long-term investors, but it is not for amateurs and it is not without risks.
5. You might invest some of your savings in T-bills or other short-term investments but only a smallish portion.
6. Long-term bonds will be especially poor performers, since bond yields have nowhere to go but up, and this would create capital losses. This includes real return bonds.
7. Your best bet for a 5 percent annual return is to invest in equity funds, risky as they are.
8. A 60-40 asset mix is probably better than 50-50 in the case of retirees with average risk tolerance.

CHAPTER 8

What if You See a Black Swan?

Black Swans

The Thompsons' retirement planning was sabotaged by 5th-percentile investment returns. In Part II, we will find a way to salvage the situation with the very same returns.

In the meantime, readers might wonder whether they should worry about even poorer returns. I'm thinking about returns at the 1st-percentile level or even worse. They are hard to study, precisely because they are so rare. Monte Carlo simulations might be good at modelling investment returns between the 5th percentile and the 95th percentile, but when you go deeper into the tails of the distribution, it is a different matter.

Nassim Taleb coined the name "black swan" for highly unusual events. The fact that he did so just before the 2008 global financial meltdown made him famous. In Taleb's definition, a black swan possesses the following three characteristics:

1. It is totally unexpected since nothing in our experience could have led us to predict its occurrence.

2. It carries an extreme impact.
3. Even though it is totally unexpected, it is human nature to try to explain the event in hindsight and to rationalize why we should have seen it coming.

The global financial meltdown of 2008–2009 qualifies as a black swan. Perhaps 9/11 does as well, though most of the bear market at the time was caused by the bursting of the dot-com bubble a year earlier. What about the extraordinary scenario that began to unfold in early 2020?

The COVID-19 Pandemic of 2020

In February 2020, I was busy working on revisions to this second edition of *Retirement Income for Life*. I had come to the chapter on investment risk in the first edition, where I showed a photo of a black swan with the caption "When will we see the next one?" By early March, it was clear that something extraordinary was happening around the world. My first thought was to add a footnote to the effect that "the 2020 bear market triggered by the COVID-19 outbreak might just be the next black swan."

Along with the rest of the world, I had a greater appreciation of what was happening by early April, and it was evident that a simple footnote would not suffice. Even though it is still too early to know how severe it will be or how long it will last, the COVID-19 pandemic appears destined to have a more profound effect on our lives than any other event in living memory.*

If you judge it only by the number of people who had been directly affected by this coronavirus as of April 2020, this pandemic doesn't seem significant enough to qualify as a black swan. As of April 14, two million cases had been reported, and while that sounds like a large number, most of them were mild with a full recovery expected. Yes, there were also 126,000 deaths worldwide, which is a tragedy for those who lost a loved one, but that number is comparable to the annual death toll from the regular winter flu season. It pales in comparison to the Spanish influenza outbreak of

---

* I wrote this section in mid-April 2020 and haven't modified it since.

1918–1920 which killed at least 50 million people at a time when the world population was a quarter of what it is today.

The financial and human impact of the pandemic, however, was anything but modest. It was clear to developed nations early on that the number of cases and deaths had the potential to grow exponentially for many months. There was talk of up to 70 percent of the entire population in some parts of the world eventually becoming infected with the virus. Draconian steps were taken to slow down its spread.

Companies started to curtail their operations. Some people could still work from home, but vast numbers were laid off. The speed with which the global economy declined surpassed even the Great Depression. By April, the unemployment rate in the US had soared to 14.7 percent (it had been under 4 percent in the fourth quarter of 2019). Former Federal Reserve chair Janet Yellen declared that second quarter GDP was on track to decline by at least 30 percent. In Canada, more than a million people lost their jobs in March alone. This dwarfed the previous one-month record for job losses (which occurred in January 2009) by a factor of eight!

The April 8, 2020, issue of the *Guardian* noted, "With each passing day, the 2008 financial crisis increasingly looks like a mere dry run for today's economic catastrophe. The short-term collapse in global output now under way already seems likely to rival or exceed that of any recession in the last 150 years."

The Day the Earth Stood Still

Grim as the economic data is, the way that people's lives were changing was even more dramatic. Grandparents could no longer visit their grandchildren. Major office buildings that used to be teeming with thousands of workers were virtually empty. Schools and churches shut down as did dentists' offices, barbershops, and most retail stores. Grocery stores were the exception, but with access limited to enable shoppers to maintain a two-metre distance from each other. Elective surgeries were cancelled. People stopped buying or selling houses. Professional sports were put on an indefinite pause. Museums, theatres, and other venues also shut down. Restaurants closed their doors, apart from takeout. Car traffic dwindled to a fraction of what it was in normal times. It became unusual to hear an airplane in the sky as up to 90 percent of air travel was cancelled. People still walked in their neighbourhoods, but even that became difficult as everyone was leery of their fellow pedestrians. Life imitated art as the world resembled a science-fiction movie of some dystopian future.

With this as a backdrop, it is no surprise that the capital markets exhibited unprecedented behaviour. Long-term government bond yields in Canada and the US fell below 1 percent for the first time ever. The price of West Texas Intermediate oil for May delivery actually went negative. In 2008, the price per barrel had been as high as US $145.

Stock markets also swooned in spectacular fashion. The S&P 500 index fell 30 percent from its all-time high in a mere 22 days in the first quarter of 2020. It had never fallen that far that fast before. It did recover somewhat by mid-April but, as I write this, it is still an open question as to whether the downward trend is over. From the perspective of how people everywhere conducted their everyday lives and how financial markets were affected, the coronavirus pandemic easily qualifies as a black swan of epic proportions.

> **S & P 500** is an index that tracks the performance of 500 large U.S. companies.

How to Deal with Black Swans

By the time you read this, the pandemic will probably be over. It might even be a distant memory. The reason it is highlighted here is that it provides a rare, real-life example of the difficult choices that investors must make when they are caught in the middle of a black swan event. At this point, no one knows how long or severe the recession will be or how far stocks will eventually fall. If you are a retiree or are nearing retirement, how do you protect what remains of your nest egg during this extraordinary period?

In the original edition of this book, I posed the question of whether fear of another market meltdown (like 2008) is reason enough to steer clear of stocks in retirement. At the time, my answer was an emphatic no, but perhaps the issue is not quite so black and white. It is one thing to dismiss black swans when they are hypothetical future events or distant memories; it is another when you see one forming before your very eyes.

Consider the Thompsons and imagine that the pandemic has not yet happened. If they felt it would be a complete disaster to lose all their savings and live off just CPP and OAS, then a 5th-percentile scenario is something to be avoided at all costs. A black swan event would be just that much worse. They would have done well to put all their RRIF assets in a savings account as described in Chapter 7.

But what if you were already invested in stocks at the time the pandemic started and saw your retirement savings fall by 10 or 15 percent? Since the markets could conceivably fall another 15 percent or more, what should you do with your portfolio?

I concede there are no cut and dried answers to this question, but I can at least help you to analyze your choices. The first decision is to gauge how far stocks might eventually fall if you stay fully invested. Perhaps history can provide some insights.

Bear markets, which are defined as a decline in a stock market index of 20 percent or more, are nothing new. If we look at the S&P 500 index, there have been ten bear markets in the past 70 years (not counting the current one), so we can expect one to occur every six or seven years on average. In spite of them, stock investors have been richly rewarded for taking risk.

If bear markets all evolved in the same fashion, we wouldn't have to be so afraid of them, but that isn't the case. Since 1950, we have witnessed two types of bear markets. Type 1 is the plain vanilla variety, the type that is usually accompanied by an economic slowdown after the economy had become overheated. Seven of the last ten bear markets fall into this category. The average decline in stocks during a type 1 bear market has been 27 percent, and the average duration has been just over ten months.

It is the type 2 bear market that causes the real pain. This type is triggered by an event that fundamentally changes our world, sometimes literally overnight. I am referring to the bear markets that occurred in:

- 1973–1974, caused by the OPEC oil price shocks;
- 2000–2002, started with the bursting of the dot-com bubble in 2000 but then made infinitely worse by the events of 9/11; and

- 2008–2009, due to the near-meltdown of the global financial markets.

The average decline during these three bear markets was 51 percent, with an average duration of 23 months. In other words, type 2 bear markets have fallen about twice as far and lasted twice as long as the type 1 variety.

Given the mind-numbing start to the coronavirus-induced bear market, the comatose global economies, and the unprecedented changes to our daily living patterns, it certainly feels like a type 2 bear market. An eventual drop of 50 percent in the stock market indices would therefore not come as a surprise. In fact, it could ultimately be much worse; in the three years following the crash of 1929, the Dow Jones fell 89.2 percent.

To be clear, the current pandemic is not enough reason to cause capital markets to collapse. As mentioned earlier, the 1918 influenza pandemic was far more deadly, yet it barely caused a blip on the stock markets of the day. It is not so much pandemics that cause markets to fall, or economies to crater, but how we react to them. So far, the reaction has been unprecedented, but given the Herculean measures countries are taking to keep their economies afloat, a fall of 50 percent seems much more likely than a Depression-era plunge of 80 percent.

This brings us back to the fundamental question of what investors should do, especially retired investors. One option is to stay fully invested and to spend modestly in the interim. This approach has stood the test of time, at least for the last three-quarters of a century. Anyone who stayed fully invested during the 2008–2009 market meltdown, for instance, was eventually rewarded. The one caveat is that this strategy will almost certainly cause investors a lot of stress in the coming months, especially for retirees and especially if the market tests new lows.

A second option is to reduce your equity holdings, hopefully by selling on an uptick in the stock markets. Then make a commitment to buy back in when the stock markets have fallen by a predetermined percentage, such as 40 percent. Such an uptick has already happened in recent weeks. As of April 14, the S&P 500 Index traded at 2791, well up from its multi-year low of 2291, which occurred in late March.

One problem with this strategy is that there may not be another uptick at the current market level. A bigger problem is that absolutely no one is consistently good at timing the market. If the stock markets do fall 50 percent (assuming that is your target), you will be hard-pressed to start buying stocks again at that point because the investment climate will never feel worse. If you wait until the recovery becomes more certain, however, you might miss the boat and never buy back in.

The third option is to take your lumps and sell your equity holdings now, with no plan to buy back in later. At least you will have avoided selling at the very bottom of the market. This might turn out to be the smartest strategy if you (a) have enough assets left to furnish the lifestyle you want in retirement and (b) literally cannot afford to see stocks going much lower. Just be ready to handle the possible chagrin. Markets never stay low forever, and you may well come to regret being on the sidelines when the recovery inevitably begins.

To conclude this chapter, I should emphasize that my aim is to protect retirees from challenging situations, including 5th-percentile investment scenarios. As we will see in Part II, this is quite possible. Dealing with black swan events is another matter. The evasive actions described above, coupled with the enhancements described later, will mitigate the financial impact of a black swan, but you are unlikely to escape its effects entirely.

Takeaways

1. Black swan events can lead to unusually severe bear markets that can disrupt your retirement planning.
2. The last 70 years of bear markets suggest it is best to stay fully invested during a market downturn, but a bear market brought on by a black swan event may be different.
3. You might consider reducing your equity exposure on the way down but only if you are prepared to miss the subsequent market recovery.

CHAPTER 9

Where the Thompsons Stand

In Chapters 4 through 7, we uncovered several shortcomings in the Thompsons' decumulation strategy. None of these would have been fatal had their investments performed adequately, but that wasn't the case. Because of 5th-percentile investment returns, the Thompsons ran out of money with many years to go in their retirement.

With each flaw we uncovered, we took corrective measures, which are summarized below:

1. Having the Thompsons create a rainy-day reserve to blunt the impact of future spending shocks.
2. Fixing their income pattern in retirement by filling the shortfall in income before Susan's OAS pension started and by having income in their later retirement years rise in line with their needs.
3. Switching from a 50-50 asset mix to 60-40.

The result of all these changes is shown in Figure 9.1.

Figure 9.1. The Thompsons are now ready for enhancements

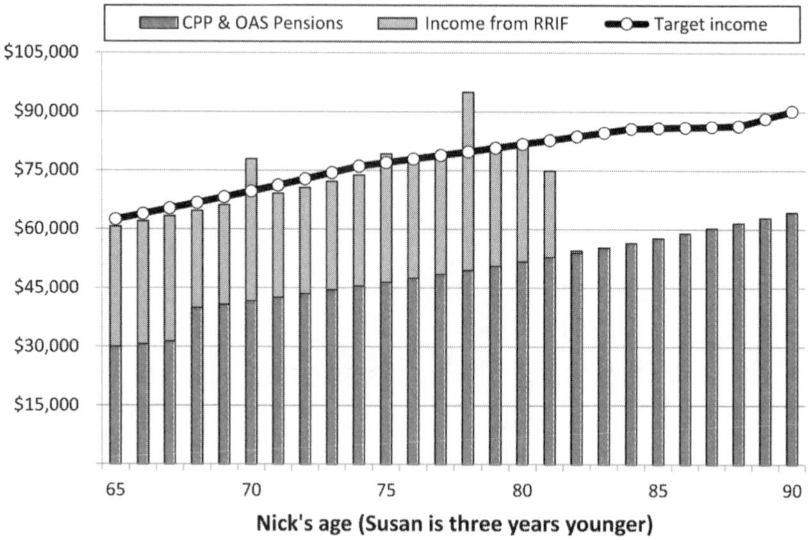

| CPP & OAS Pensions | Income from RRIF | Target income |

Nick's age (Susan is three years younger)

This is the same as Figure 5.2 except the asset mix is now 60-40.

Getting Ready for the Enhancements

Based on the chart, it would seem the Thompsons have taken a step backward. After adopting the three corrective measures, they are running out of money just as early as they did in our very first projection. But things are about to get much better.

In Part II, I will take the Thompsons through a series of five enhancements that will erase the income gaps that develop in their later years. Furthermore, this miracle will happen without assuming that the Thompsons got luckier with their investments, drew less income at the outset, or somehow avoided the spending shocks. No, the better outcome will simply be a matter of putting the following principles into practice:

> Enhancement 1 — Reducing transaction costs: Some expenses are unavoidable, but when it comes to investing, they can be reduced significantly without hurting your investment returns.
>
> Enhancements 2 and 3 — Transferring your risks to others: You want to eliminate the chances of a truly catastrophic

outcome. You can do this by transferring some of the risk to institutions that are better equipped to handle it. This includes government and insurance companies.

Enhancement 4 — Using an actuary's expertise in determining how much income to draw: When it comes to drawing income, you face two problems. The first one is to set the initial income in year 1 at the right level. The second problem is adjusting that amount on a regular basis as your financial circumstances change. Enhancement 4 addresses these problems.

Enhancement 5 — Having a backstop if all else fails: While it is highly unlikely, the previous four enhancements *can* fail. That is when Enhancement 5 is called for. It enables you to tap other sources of wealth if you find yourself short of money late in retirement.

Going Through the Checklist

No doubt you would like to dive straight into the enhancements, but first let's ensure you are starting from the right place. Ideally, you are taking all the following steps to prepare for retirement:

1. **Finish paying off the mortgage on your house by the time you retire.** If you still have a sizeable mortgage, you might not be retirement-ready. Yes, the interest rate on mortgages is low these days, but the risk-free interest you are earning on bank accounts or fixed income investments in your portfolio is lower still.

2. **Pay off your credit cards each month.** The worst thing you can do is carry over unpaid balances into the following month. The credit card companies are charging you interest at close to 20 percent a year.

3. **Don't use a home equity line of credit to supplement your regular spending needs.** It is always a good idea to live

within your means, but in retirement it is essential. Using a home equity line of credit to augment your spending suggests you are not living within your means, and this is dangerous.

4. **Encourage your children to be independent.** Ideally, you and your spouse are the only people you need to worry about after you retire. It is quite possible you are still helping your kids out financially. In my opinion, this is suboptimal, but it is up to you how you spend your money as long as you live within your budget.

5. **Ensure your investments are not locked in.** Some mutual funds come with deferred sales charges (DSCs). The purpose of these is to pay the mutual fund salesperson upfront, but the result is not at all favourable for you as an investor since it takes away your freedom to act. If you have some money tied up in one-year GICs, that is acceptable, but the period shouldn't be longer than that.

6. **Make sure your marriage is solid.** A break-up is always difficult, but after retirement it is financially devastating. If it happens before retirement, you might at least be able to take some steps to secure your financial well-being, such as working a little longer and saving more.

Now that we have established our game plan, let's move on to Part II!

Takeaway

1. Before embarking on the enhancements, you should get your finances in order by going through the checklist.

PART II

A Five-Part Solution

I introduce five ways in which the Thompsons can enhance their decumulation strategy. The goal is to make their money last a lifetime, even if their investment returns are poor.

CHAPTER 10

Enhancement 1: Reducing Fees

You will recall that Nick and Susan invested their RRIF assets in mutual funds and paid a total annual fee of 1.8 percent. This level of fee, which is also known as the **management expense ratio (MER)**, is fairly typical if one invests in a blend of actively managed equity and fixed income mutual funds in the retail market.

When your total expected annual return is just 5 percent or so, you shouldn't be giving up 1.8 percent in fees. That would leave you with a return of only 1 or 2 percent a year after inflation, less if your investments don't do too well!

Management expense ratio (MER) is the total percentage of assets the investment company charges you in a given year to cover investment, administrative, and other sales-related charges. For example, an MER of 1.8 percent on assets of $500,000 results in annual expenses of $9,000. In the case of mutual funds, these fees are quietly deducted from the assets. Various series of funds are available from

each company with different fee levels depending on
(a) how much you are investing and (b) whether you are
working with a professional advisor who charges you an
additional fee.

Enhancement 1 involves bringing the MER down from 1.8 percent to 0.6 percent a year. As described later on, there are at least a couple of ways this can be accomplished. The way you choose depends on the extent of your investment knowledge and how much time you want to spend managing your money.

We will assume that Nick and Susan go with a robo-advisor and end up paying 0.6 percent a year, including both the robo-advisor fee as well as the cost of the advisor's exchange-traded funds (ETFs).

The ETFs I have in mind are passively managed investments, meaning that they track an external index such as the S&P/TSX index. ETFs make no attempt to beat the market, which is just as well since most active managers fail to do so but charge a hefty fee to try. ETFs are increasingly popular because the fees tend to be much lower than is the case with active management. In addition, ETFs are easy to buy and sell.

Passive management in an investment context means an
investment that is meant to mimic an index that represents
the entire market or some subset of the market. There is
no attempt to beat the market with passively managed
funds. The alternative is active management, whereby the
manager regularly buys and sells securities in an effort to beat
the market.

The robo-advisor helps Nick and Susan put together a simple ETF portfolio as shown in Table 10.1. (I should add that the ETF examples shown in the table could easily have come from a different company. Blackrock and BMO are excellent institutions, but I am not claiming that they are better or worse than their competitors.)

Table 10.1. Fees for a typical ETF portfolio

Asset class	Example of an ETF for that asset class	% of total portfolio	MER
Canadian stocks	BMO S&P/TSX Capped Composite Index ETF	20%	0.06%
US stocks	iShares Core S&P 500 ETF	20%	0.10%
International stocks	iShares Core MSCI EAFE IMI Index ETF	20%	0.22%
Canadian bonds	iShares ESG Canadian Aggregate Bond Index ETF	35%	0.20%
Cash equivalent	BMO Ultra Short-Term Bond ETF	5%	0.17%
Total portfolio		100%	0.1545%

The above portfolio has an annual MER of just 0.1545 percent. Yes, that is less than one-sixth of 1 percent! In addition, their robo-advisor charged another 0.4 percent, bringing the total annual fee to a little under 0.6 percent. It could have been even less than that since at least one robo-advisor charges just 0.25 percent a year.

On the other hand, the total annual cost could have easily topped 0.6 percent if Nick and Susan had chosen a traditional advisor who charges a higher annual fee, such as 1 percent a year. They might have taken this route if they needed a little more hand-holding but, frankly, I don't think that the function of setting and maintaining one's asset mix is worth more than 0.4 percent a year. I am not saying that the model asset mix in Table 10.1 is optimal, but it is at least adequate. No one could tell you for sure whether another asset mix would be better.

If Nick and Susan did decide to go to a traditional advisor, they should have no qualms about pushing back on fees. An advisor was charging a friend of mine more than 2 percent a year (including underlying charges for the mutual funds). When I suggested to my friend that he consider a robo-advisor, the advisor offered to slash the total cost to just 0.9 percent, with no change in the portfolio or in the service level he provided!

By the way, the Thompsons' robo-advisor will have to engage in some buying and selling of the ETFs to keep the same asset mix over time. It is not uncommon to see one asset class (such as Canadian stocks) rise in value much faster than another (such as Canadian bonds), and if the portfolio is not rebalanced, the asset mix will quietly drift. This is not only dangerous; it is a missed opportunity. The Canadian Institute of Actuaries (CIA) confirms the benefits of rebalancing the asset mix on a regular basis (such as once a quarter). Over the long run, this practice can add up to 50 basis points to the annual return, which is as close as you will ever come to a free lunch in the investment world.

Do ETFs Perform as Well?

You might be wondering if Nick and Susan are giving something up by paying so little for investment management. It defies the notion of getting what you pay for. Can passive management using ETFs really match the performance of active fund managers?

You would think there would be a clear and concise answer to this question, but that isn't the case. Certainly, the professional investment managers will claim to add value, but they are hard-pressed to show it over the long term.

Burton Malkiel famously claimed that a monkey throwing darts could select stocks as well as investment managers.* A serious investment journal tested this claim once and reported the results in a paper that was published in 2013.[1] The authors found that inverting the algorithms behind popular, well-established stock-picking strategies provided equal or better performance. They further concluded that the same is true with any random stock-selection strategy. In other words, you could follow a given approach or you could do precisely the opposite, and in the long run, the result would essentially be the same!

A good source of hard data on the subject is the SPIVA Canada Scorecard, which is published every six months. SPIVA stands for Standard and Poor's Index Versus Active and as the name suggests, SPIVA reports actively managed investment funds versus their benchmarks. Table 10.2

---

* Malkiel is the author of the brilliant book *A Random Walk Down Wall Street*, first published in 1973 by W.W. Norton & Company.

shows the percentage of managers in each major category who outperformed their respective benchmark in calendar years 2016 and 2018.

Table 10.2. Percent of managers outperforming their benchmark

	2016	2018
Canadian equity	17.3%	23.1%
Canadian dividend and income	19.4%	34.8%
US equity	28.4%	21.4%
Global equity	24.1%	22.5%

Source: SPIVA Canada scorecard

I chose 2016 and 2018 as examples of years when the markets did especially well and especially poorly, respectively. The obvious message from Table 10.2 is that the average investment manager cannot consistently beat the index in good times or in bad. This is quite astounding given that the managers do a great deal of research on the economy as well as on individual companies and try to do their best to avoid the losers.

The years 2016 and 2018 are not anomalies. As SPIVA Canada points out in their Scorecard report, *more than nine funds in ten* underperformed their benchmarks over the most recent ten-year period.

While the SPIVA findings are rather compelling, other sources show the median active fund manager doing a little better. For instance, Morneau Shepell maintains a quarterly survey that they call the *Performance Universe of Pension Managers' Pooled Funds*. This is available online for free at morneaushepell.com by clicking on Knowledge & Insights. The most recent survey shows the median fund manager more or less matches the benchmark return. While this seems to conflict with SPIVA, there are three differences between the two sources. In the case of the Morneau Shepell survey:

1. The fund manager's fees are not included; these can be significant.
2. Not all fund managers are in the survey; it seems plausible that the ones who are performing especially poorly decline to participate.

3. There is no correction for survivorship bias. This term refers to the fact that the survey shows only the funds that are still there at the end of the period, i.e., the survivors. There may have been more funds at the beginning of the period that dropped out or even closed their doors because of poor results.

At this point, most readers should be convinced that active management doesn't add value or at least not enough value to justify the fees. But let's be fair and give the active managers one more chance. Let's suppose for a moment that the *average* active manager doesn't add value but maybe the top 10 percent of managers do. Maybe it's just a question of finding the few managers who are consistently outstanding and putting your money with them.

Alas, there is no proof that some investment management firms are consistently better than their peers. Consider the managers of domestic equity funds who were in the top quartile as of September 2017. According to a SPIVA Canada report entitled *Does Past Performance Matter? The Persistence Scorecard*, only 8 percent of them were in the top quartile two years later. This result is barely different from random chance, which would predict that 6.25 percent (25 percent of one-quarter) would still be in the top quartile in the later period.

What is remarkable is that the investment management community has managed to convince so many investors that they can "do better" than the benchmarks. (As an aside, investors tend to exhibit the same unfounded optimism about beating the odds, as do newlyweds who ignore dismal statistics on divorce.) The data suggests they cannot, and the reason comes down to the efficiency of the markets; i.e., the markets reflect all available information in the current prices of securities. Moreover, the markets do this so quickly that fund managers cannot act fast enough to take advantage of a temporary mispricing of a particular security.

Impact of Reducing Fees

If Nick and Susan reduced their investment management fees down to 0.6 percent from the outset (instead of 1.8 percent), Figure 10.1 shows how

Figure 10.1. After Enhancement 1, reducing investment fees

Nick's age (Susan is three years younger)

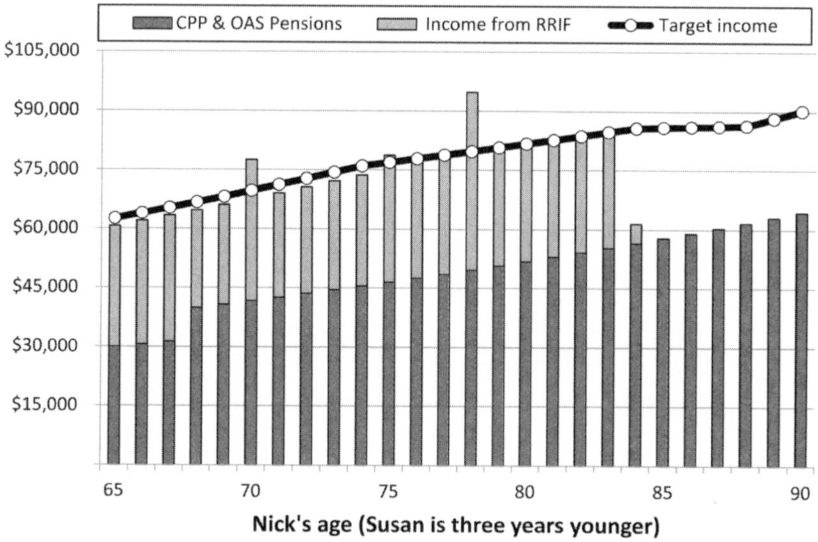

This is the same as Figure 9.1 except investment fees are reduced to 0.6% a year. RRIF income lasts nearly three years longer as a result.

much more income they would be able to generate. Simply reducing fees adds nearly three more years of RRIF income.

It is important to note that Nick and Susan enjoy this improved result without getting investment returns that are any better than they had in the previous scenarios; they are simply giving up less of their money to financial advisors.

Although the financial picture has improved for Nick and Susan as a direct result of reducing their investment fees, their actual income still falls well short of their income target in their latter years. The next enhancement will eliminate most of the shortfall.

Takeaways

1. Reducing investment fees can significantly increase one's retirement income.

2. Actively managed funds are more expensive than passively managed funds, like ETFs, but with no evidence that they add value when you take fees into account.
3. Using passively managed ETFs, the total annual investment fee can be brought down to about 0.45 to 0.6 percent if you use a robo-advisor, less if you do it all yourself.

CHAPTER 11

Enhancement 2:
Transfer Risk to the Government

Almost every big bank survey confirms that the biggest concern among retirees (after their health) is outliving their savings. And for good reason, as we have seen that even responsible people like the Thompsons can lose their entire nest egg long before they die. Enhancement 1 helps Nick and Susan stretch their retirement dollars almost three more years, but that isn't enough to close the income gap. They still end up with only their CPP and OAS pensions by the time Susan is 81 (and my mother will tell you that's not old).

The trouble is that the Thompsons are getting too much of their income from unreliable sources. What would really help is having more income that they can count on no matter what. The CPP pension is a great example of the type of income they should want: it is fully indexed to inflation and is sure to be paid. The only problem is that it's not nearly enough to meet the needs of a middle-income household. The maximum amount payable to an individual at age 65 is just over $14,100 a year.*

---

* This is the maximum payable to someone who reaches age 65 in 2020.

But what if you could increase your CPP pension by more than 40 percent? Wouldn't it be nice to receive a bigger CPP pension that is both inflation-protected and paid for life? Even if worse comes to worst and your personal savings run out at some point, you still have the larger CPP payments to dull the pain.

There is only one catch. To get the larger payments, you must postpone your CPP pension until a later age, and this does not go over well with most people. Government statistics show that almost no one likes the idea of waiting to get their CPP benefit; only 1 percent or so of all CPP recipients postpone the start of their CPP payments until age 70, which is the latest starting age. As for the people in that exclusive 1 percent group, I wonder how many started their CPP pension late simply because they didn't get around to completing the necessary paperwork sooner!

Enhancement 2 involves waiting until age 70 to start collecting CPP pension. I will show just how effective this enhancement can be (at least in most situations), but first let's go over the basic rules for how CPP pensions are calculated.

How CPP Pension Is Calculated

Your CPP pension is based on the contributions you make. From ages 18 to 65, you are required to contribute to the CPP in any year that you earn at least $3,500 with any one employer. You contribute only on employment earnings between $3,500 and a ceiling that approximates the national average wage. In 2020, that ceiling is $58,700.

There are 47 potential years of contributions between ages 18 and 65, but you need to contribute the maximum amount in only 39 of those years to receive the maximum CPP pension at age 65. In other words, you get to drop out eight years of low or no earnings for purposes of the pension calculation. The dropout period is even longer in special cases, such as for people who stayed at home to raise young children. If you have employment earnings in the years that you want to drop out, you are still required to contribute, even if doing so doesn't change your pension.

If you retire early, you can start to receive your CPP pension as early as age 60. In this case, the amount you receive is reduced by 7.2 percent for each year that you start your CPP pension before age 65. At age 60, you would therefore collect just 64 percent of what you receive at 65. (This is only an approximation since the dropout rules mentioned above might affect the percentage slightly.)

If you start your CPP pension late, the reverse happens. Your CPP pension grows by 8.4 percent for each year that you wait beyond age 65 (but only up until age 70). If you start CPP at age 70, the benefit is at least 42 percent higher than if you start it at age 65. I say "at least" because the increase could be more than 42 percent if you keep on contributing to CPP after 65. Another way that the increase can exceed 42 percent is if the average national wage rises faster than general price inflation. If wage increases beat price increases by 1 percent a year, your CPP pension at 70 would be almost 50 percent more than if you started to receive it at 65.

These are the basic rules. There are some quirks in the rules that affect survivor benefits and whether you have to contribute after 65. The details are covered in Appendix D.

Impact of a Bigger CPP Pension

Based on his earnings record, Nick was entitled to 90 percent of the maximum CPP pension at 65. This works out to about $12,700 a year if he starts CPP at age 65. If he waits until age 70, it will be at least $18,000 and, as mentioned above, it could be even more than that if average wages in Canada climb faster than price inflation.

Susan was entitled to 70 percent of the maximum, which equals $9,880 at 65 (rounded up) and is at least $14,020 if she starts payments at 70. Between the two of them, Nick and Susan can look forward to more than $32,000 of CPP pension starting at age 70. If they do wait until 70, though, they will need to make up for the lost income between ages 65 and 70, and the only way they can do that is to draw down their RRIF balance more rapidly.

It can be stressful to watch your RRIF balance shrinking, especially if investment returns are poor, but the Thompsons need to have faith. It is counterintuitive, but in the long run their RRIF assets will last longer if they adopt Enhancement 2 than if they don't. This is because the RRIF drawdowns slow dramatically once their larger CPP pensions kick in at age

70. You have to tell yourself not to worry about getting less income from the RRIF because the greater income from CPP more than makes up for it.

Figure 11.1 shows how this would look. Before age 70, the green bars represent only OAS pension, but those bars more than double in size when Nick is 70 and starts to collect CPP. They jump again when Susan turns 70 (at which point Nick is 73). From that point on, the green bars are much higher than they were in Figure 10.1, thanks to the bigger CPP pension.

Figure 11.1. After Enhancement 2, deferring CPP to 70

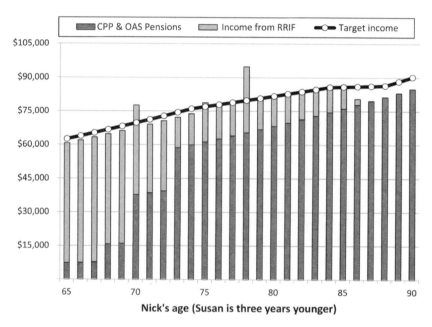

This is the same as Figure 10.1 except CPP is deferred until age 70. The income gap at later ages has shrunk dramatically.

Enhancement 2 greatly improves the overall financial situation for Nick and Susan. They now meet their income target for another two years but, more importantly, their income gap in the remaining years is much smaller than it was before Enhancement 2. In fact, the gap has shrunk by about 75 percent to the point that it is barely noticeable. This is what a bigger CPP pension does for them.

The benefits from Enhancement 2 don't stop there. Investment risk is significantly reduced because the Thompsons are no longer relying so heavily on their savings. They drew their RRIF down more quickly and replaced the uncertain RRIF income with much more secure income from the Canada Pension Plan.

Because CPP is payable for life, the risk of living too long and running out of money is practically eliminated. If Nick died at age 88, for instance, Susan could look forward to receiving nearly $50,000 just from CPP and OAS alone. This is nearly $10,000 a year more than before Enhancement 2. Admittedly, these are inflated dollars because Nick will not be 88 for another 23 years, but if we back out inflation in this calculation, Susan still gets nearly $30,000 of CPP and OAS income in present-day dollars.

Enhancement 2 looks almost too good to be true. With it, Nick and Susan can draw their target income for longer and almost close the income gap, even if they exhaust the assets in their RRIF. The reason this enhancement works so well is that the Canada Pension Plan is absorbing a great deal of the investment risk and longevity risk and is doing so on terms that are very favourable to the retiree.

So why are there so few takers? This question deserves a chapter of its own.

Takeaways

1. Deferring CPP pension to age 70 forces you to draw down your RRIF assets (or other assets) more quickly before age 70, but those same assets last longer because the CPP pension from age 70 and on is so much bigger.
2. Enhancement 2 greatly reduces the income gap at older ages for middle-income couples like the Thompsons.

CHAPTER 12

Why So Few People Defer
Their CPP Pension

To an actuary, Enhancement 2 represents a dream come true. It reduces investment and longevity risks and increases the actuarial value of the pension at the same time. So why do so few retirees postpone their CPP until 70? Equally curious, why do so few financial planners endorse it?

Based on the many comments from people who have read my articles on the subject in *The Globe and Mail* and the *National Post*, I think I know most of the reasons why the take-up rate is so low. These reasons fall into three categories:

1. Just plain irrational
2. Rational but not valid once you know all the facts
3. Valid in special situations

I will start with the reasons that are most easily dismissed and work my way up from there.

Irrational Reasons Given for Taking CPP Early

The first reason is often mentioned by retirees and even by financial advisors. These people say that they start their CPP pensions early because they want to spend their money while they are still young. At first blush, this may sound reasonable but in fact it is totally bogus. Don't get me wrong; I am all for people spending a little more money in their early retirement years when they are most likely to enjoy it. It's just that those extra dollars do not need to come from CPP.

Instead of taking their CPP pension early, retirees could simply withdraw more money from their RRIF or some other source of income they might have. If people really want to spend more while they're young and still have some money left over when they are much older, deferring CPP is the best way to make this happen.

Another irrational reason for not deferring CPP, and by far the one I hear most often, is the "bird in the hand" argument. People tell me they don't want to postpone their CPP payments because they fear they might die early and not get full value from the Canada Pension Plan as a result. A comment I saw online following one of my articles said, "Imagine how mad you'd be if you died and the government kept your money."

Allow me to point out the obvious: if you die early, you have bigger worries than getting shortchanged on your CPP pension. Like not breathing. Your bigger concern should be what happens if you live *longer* than you expected because you will still be around to regret a bad decision!

Rational but Not Valid

Some reasons for not wanting to defer CPP may seem quite rational to the layperson but ultimately prove not to be valid when the facts are fully laid out. The following reasons fit this description.

Many people are not even aware they *can* defer CPP or how deferral can help them. When you are approaching age 65, the CPP administration office will send you an impressive package that outlines your CPP pension entitlement and asks you to complete an application form to start your CPP payments. The wording of the form practically assumes that you will choose to start your CPP pension by age 65. Besides, when you get an official-looking, personalized document from the government, the knee-jerk reaction is to follow instructions and send back the completed forms. But that doesn't make it right!

The second reason is more esoteric. We have a hard time envisioning a later starting age for our retirement benefits because society continues to reinforce the notion that age 65 is somehow magical. That used to be the age of mandatory retirement, the time when you could expect a gold watch and then be shown the door. Those days are gone, but the magic remains. Age 65 is still the age when (a) you pay less to get into the movie theatre or take public transit, (b) your prescription drugs are paid for by the government, and (c) you can start to receive OAS pension. It is also the *latest* age that pensions from defined benefit pension plans from an employer can start (assuming you stopped working). For all these intangible and somewhat irrelevant reasons, it is the age when you figure you should be starting your CPP pension.

Third, many financial advisors encourage their clients to start their CPP pension as soon as possible and to hold off on spending their own savings. The apparent reason for this advice is that the monies in an RRSP or a RRIF are not subject to income tax until they are withdrawn. It would therefore seem like a good idea to keep the RRSP or RRIF balance intact for as long as possible. As Figure 11.1 showed us, however, this reasoning does not stand up to closer scrutiny.

There is also a cynical explanation for such advice; it stems from the fact that most advisors are remunerated based on a percentage of assets. Understandably, they do not want to see those assets dwindling too quickly! While I wouldn't want to presume this is what motivates your own advisor, you should at least be aware that your advisor's compensation might be clouding their judgment, at least on a subconscious level.

I would like to think that most financial advisors genuinely try to do the best for their clients. If they are telling new retirees to start CPP early, it may be because they have underpriced the **actuarial present value** of deferring CPP pension until 70.

Actuarial present value is how actuaries try to take into account all the information they have about a benefit and express it as a single number. That number represents the amount that would need to be set aside today to fund that benefit. It is basically a measure of overall value all captured in one number, just like a golfer's handicap.

The second last reason in this category has been circulating for many years, and while it is mentioned less often these days, it still comes up from time to time. Some people want to start CPP early because they are afraid the Canada Pension Plan will not be around for them if they wait too long to collect.

For someone who doesn't know how the governance of the CPP has evolved, this concern is understandable. The CPP was funded on a pay-as-you-go basis until 1997, which is not a stable way to fund a plan like this. In addition, some of the early investments made with CPP contributions were politically motivated and didn't inspire confidence that the best interests of the participants were being taken into account. For these reasons, it was understandable that people in the 1990s worried about the long-term sustainability of the plan.

Fortunately, major changes were made to how the CPP is run. Contribution rates were increased from 6 percent of covered pay in 1997 to 9.9 percent in 2003. This increase built up the fund assets and stabilized the contribution rate over the longer term. At the same time, an independent body (known as the CPPIB) was established to ensure that fund investments were based on sound principles instead of politics.

CPPIB stands for Canada Pension Plan Investment Board. This is one of the largest investment institutions in the world, with large infrastructure investments extending around the globe.

In addition, the chief actuary of the Canada Pension Plan makes sophisticated long-term projections of demographics and assets, taking into account all the salient factors: investment returns, immigration, birth rates, employment rates, retirement ages, mortality rates, and so on. These projections show that the current contribution rate is sustainable over the next 75 years and more. Even if a funding deficit developed, the contribution increase needed to pay for it would be small enough to be manageable. Politicians would almost certainly act to increase contributions rather than cut benefits. With such a sound governance structure in place, I have no worries about the future of the CPP.

By contrast, if you were an American and were relying on Social Security benefits in 20 years' time, I would say you have some reason to worry. US Social Security is funded on a pay-as-you-go basis, which requires ever-higher contributions as the working-age population matures and the number of retirees grows. Based on government projections of contributions and benefits, the amount of money left in the fund by 2034 will not be enough to make full payments. This is a real problem, given that Social Security does not have the legal right to borrow and American politicians do not seem to be able to bring themselves to increase taxes. It therefore seems the US Social Security system is on a collision course, but this doesn't affect the CPP.

You would think that having a shorter-than-average life expectancy would be a good reason not to wait until 70 to collect CPP. This is true if both spouses have sound medical reasons why they expect to die young, but that is a rather rare situation. If just one spouse dies at a youngish age, it might still make sense to wait until 70 to collect CPP. This scenario is explored in Chapter 17.

Finally, there is a purely emotional reason why you may find yourself unable to wait until 70 to take CPP. If you are like many people, your sense of self-worth may be intertwined with your financial worth. For most of your working life, you were saving to improve your financial status. It would have been a comfort to watch your RRSP account balance growing steadily. Drawing down your personal assets in retirement is hard to do because it is a grim reminder not only of your dwindling influence in this life but also of your own mortality. Drawing down assets *more quickly*, as we would have to do under Enhancement 2, compounds the difficulty. This explains why people might be *reluctant* to adopt Enhancement 2, but it is not a good reason to reject it. We shouldn't care whether one particular source of income gets depleted more quickly than another. We should care only about how much income we can count on from all sources combined.

Valid Reasons Not to Defer CPP in Special Cases

Having dismissed most of the reasons for not deferring CPP, I will concede that it is sometimes better to start your CPP pension when you retire rather than waiting until 70. Consider carefully whether any of the following situations apply to you.

First, you need to have enough money to make Enhancement 2 work. Nick and Susan had a nest egg of $600,000, which turned out to be enough to tide them over until age 70. What if a couple had only $375,000, though? Figure 12.1 shows what would happen if they tried to defer their CPP until 70.

This couple is still better off deferring their CPP pension, but the situation is now less than ideal; by trying to stay on the target income curve in the early years, they end up having too much income from age 82 and on. You might think that more income is a good thing, but only if it comes at the right time. It would be better to have it earlier in their retirement when they are more apt to enjoy it. If they drew more income from their RRIF early in their retirement, however, they wouldn't have enough money left over in their 70s.

Ultimately, Enhancement 2 is a strategy only for people with significant savings. What constitutes "significant" depends heavily on the age when they retire, whether they are single or married, and the amount of CPP pension they can expect. For the Thompsons, the threshold is about $400,000. For a single person aged 65 at retirement, it would be about half that. If the Thompsons were both just 60 when they retired (with the same CPP pensions), the threshold would be closer to $800,000.

This isn't to say that deferral of CPP beyond age 65 is a complete mistake if you possess less than the threshold amount of assets. You just might not want to defer CPP all the way until age 70. A starting age for CPP pension after 65 but before 70 could make more sense in this case.

Figure 12.1. Deferring CPP to 70 with $375,000 in assets

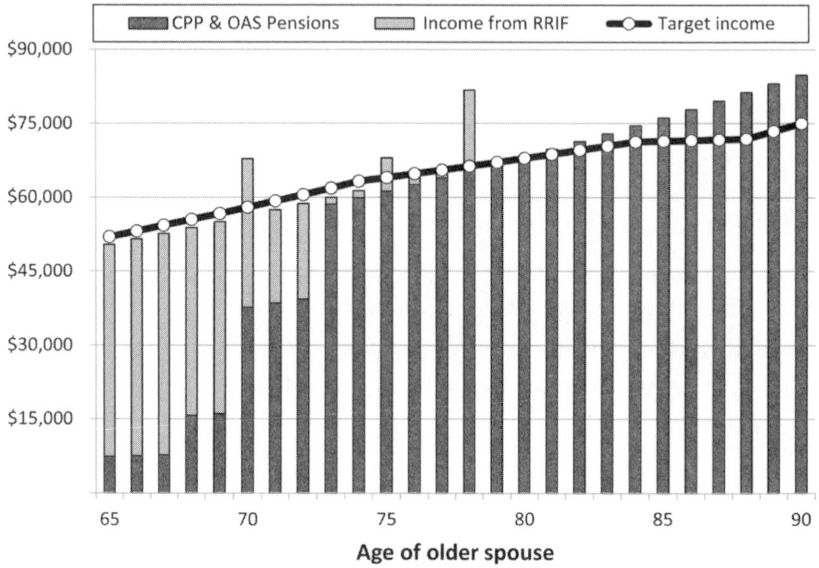

Like Figure 11.1 except this couple has only $375,000 in assets and starting income is $52,000. By deferring CPP to 70, they have too much income at 90.

The final (good) reason for not wanting to defer CPP applies if you keep on working beyond age 65 and have already earned the maximum CPP pension. Deferring CPP is less effective in this case because of a quirk in the Canada Pension Plan. You are forced to keep on contributing to the CPP even if it doesn't improve your pension.

By contrast, if you continue working past 65 but start CPP at 65, you are not forced to keep on contributing! The people who draft the rules for the Canada Pension Plan must know this can't be right. After all, they did not insert the same anomaly in their own pension plan (the federal Public Service Pension Plan)! Appendix D sets out an example of just how unfair the CPP contribution rules are.

Why Not Defer OAS, Too?

If starting one's CPP pension at age 70 is such a good idea, then why not start OAS pension at 70 as well? Many people don't realize it, but you do have the option of deferring OAS commencement until 70. There are a couple of reasons why I generally don't recommend doing it, though.

First, the actuarial adjustment you receive is lower than it is for CPP. In the case of OAS, the pension at age 70 is only 36 percent higher than at age 65, not 42 percent. The second reason is that starting CPP late is already forcing the average retiree to draw down their RRIF balance much faster than they bargained on doing. As we saw in the last section, the threshold amount of assets needed to take full advantage of CPP deferral is already rather high. It gets that much higher if the retiree decides to defer OAS pension as well.

Even if one has enough assets for deferral of OAS pension to make sense, it will make anyone with less than a million dollars in assets feel a little uncomfortable because of the accelerated drawdown of their personal assets.

The one exception applies in the case of very high earners. Those people with a six-figure income would see some or all of their entire OAS pension clawed back anyway. They might as well postpone the start date until 70 because they won't receive any value from OAS before then.

Takeaways

1. Enhancement 2 provides significant protection against investment risk as well as longevity risk.
2. There are many reasons for not deferring CPP pension to age 70, but most of them do not hold up to close scrutiny.
3. About the only good reason not to defer CPP to 70 is having insufficient assets to tide you over until CPP starts.
4. You probably will not want to defer your OAS pension unless your income after 65 is high enough to be subject to the OAS clawback rules.

CHAPTER 13

Enhancement 3:
Transfer Even More Risk

In Chapter 11, we found that deferring the start of CPP pension to 70 was a great way for retirees to transfer risk to the Canada Pension Plan. It helped Nick and Susan improve their financial situation immensely. As we will learn in this chapter, they would do well to transfer a little more risk, but this time to an insurance company.

This second risk transfer will be accomplished by using some of their RRIF or RRSP money to buy a life annuity from the insurance company. For a variety of reasons, annuities are not popular, but let's suspend judgment until we see what an annuity purchase can do for the Thompsons.

Remember, the primary purpose of a decumulation strategy is to reach your income target no matter what happens. In the case of Nick and Susan, the first two enhancements went a long way toward achieving this goal. They still do not have total financial security, however, as their RRIF money ran out when Susan was 83, leaving them short of their target income in all future years.

Under Enhancement 3, the Thompsons would use 20 percent of their RRIF — an amount equal to $120,000 — to buy a life annuity from a major life insurance company at the point of retirement. Based on current interest rates and mortality tables, the Thompsons can expect an annuity of about $6,700 a year but this amount can vary over time. This annuity would be payable for as long as they are both still alive. When one of them dies, the annual amount payable reduces to $4,467.

This form of annuity is known as a "joint and-thirds survivor" annuity since it is payable not only for the life of the person who buys the annuity but also for the life of the surviving spouse. An annuity that continues at 100 percent to the surviving spouse (instead of two-thirds) might also appeal to Nick and Susan, since it would provide better income protection for the survivor if one of them were to die very young. That protection comes at a high price, though, since a 100 percent survivor benefit is expensive. And in Chapter 17, when we see what happens if Nick dies early, we will find that an annuity that reduces by a third provides Susan with ample income protection. For these reasons, we will settle on the joint and two-thirds survivor annuity described above.

Impact of Enhancement 3

Enhancement 3 is reflected in Figure 13.1, which also includes the previous two enhancements. By purchasing the annuity, their RRIF assets drop from $600,000 to $480,000, so the RRIF produces 20 percent less income than in the previous scenario. Nevertheless, the annuity purchase helps to put Nick and Susan over the top. If you compare Figures 11.1 and 13.1, you will see that the income gap has now been closed.

What the chart does not show is that the Thompsons' income exceeds the target no matter how long they live. Moreover, the income after 90 that is coming from secure sources — CPP, OAS, and a life annuity — is more than enough to meet their income target so they don't even have to use their remaining life savings. They would never have to worry again about how the stock market is doing.

After Enhancement 3, the Thompsons are virtually immune from both investment risk and longevity risk. What made this possible is that they drew down their risky assets first, meaning the money in their RRIF that was invested in stocks and bonds.

Figure 13.1. Income after Enhancement 3, buying an annuity

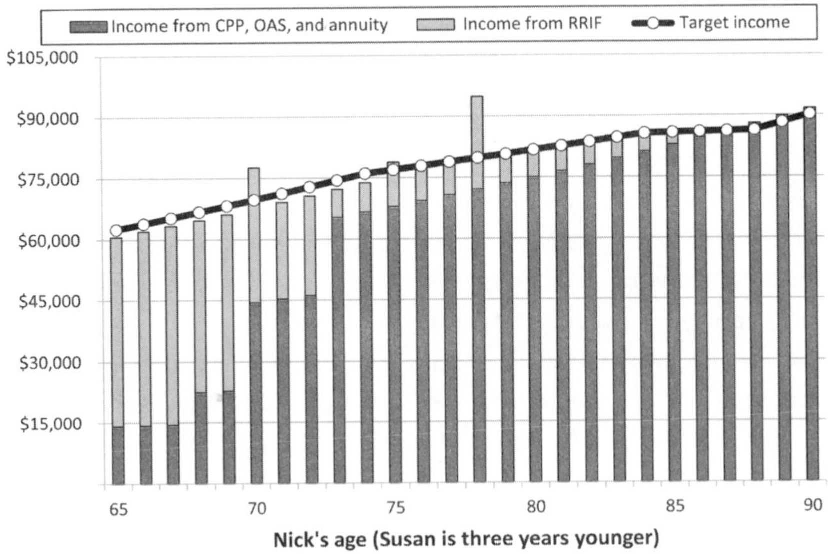

The same as Figure 11.1 except the Thompsons buy an annuity with 20% of their RRSP at retirement. The income at later ages is now closed, and they have more assets in their 90s.

Note that the annuity they are buying does not provide any inflation protection. Such an annuity is known as an **indexed annuity**. A non-indexed annuity will be worth a little less each year as inflation slowly erodes its purchasing power. You might think this is a big drawback — and indeed it would be if the Thompsons' sole source of income was the annuity — but remember that it is just one piece in the overall puzzle. The shape of each piece isn't important provided that all the pieces fit when the puzzle is finally put together, and as we just saw in Figure 13.1, the pieces fit very well.

Even if an indexed annuity made some sense, I still wouldn't recommend it. Insurance companies don't like to sell fully indexed annuities and most people don't like to buy them. As a result, indexed annuities tend to be overpriced, assuming you could find someone to sell it to you.

> An **indexed annuity** is an annuity that provides inflation protection. It increases annually in line with increases in the general inflation rate. You would be unlikely to find one where

the inflation protection isn't capped. An indexed annuity will be much more expensive than a traditional annuity that provides level annual payments.

You might be wondering where the 20 percent figure for the annuity purchase comes from. In other words, why use 20 percent of your RRIF or RRSP assets to buy an annuity versus 10 percent or 30 percent? I did try different percentages and 20 percent seemed optimal. If it is less than that in the case of the Thompsons, it doesn't fully protect them in their late 80s and beyond. If it is more, it eats into their RRIF income too much and reduces the upside potential in the likely event that the investments do better than the 5th-percentile scenario we have been assuming.

Annuities: To Buy or Not to Buy?

As we just saw, the purchase of an annuity enabled Nick and Susan to achieve virtually complete income security in retirement in spite of the spending shocks and poor investment returns. And because all their income later in retirement comes from secure sources, it will always be there for them, no matter how long they live.

So why aren't annuities more popular? Fewer than 5 percent of all people who are in a position to buy an annuity actually do so. There are many reasons for this, some good and some not so good. As it happens, most of those reasons are the same ones that people give for not deferring their CPP pension until age 70. Here is a partial list:

- Not having enough assets to make it work
- A shorter-than-usual life expectancy
- The fear of dying early and leaving money on the table (the bird-in-the-hand argument)
- Not wanting to see one's assets depleted more quickly than is absolutely necessary

In addition, some potential objections apply specifically to the question of buying an annuity. First, what if your marriage is not entirely solid? I have already recommended that the annuity be a joint and survivor form. Such an annuity, however, ties your fate to that of your spouse for the rest of time. It's great if you have a solid marriage, but it can cause some complications otherwise.

Second, the fact that you would be using 20 percent of your RRIF assets to buy the annuity ($120,000 in the case of the Thompsons) means that you would no longer be able to use that money to earn a better-than-average return on the stock market. This problem is known as opportunity cost. To get an idea of what that cost might be, consider what would have happened if Nick and Susan enjoyed a median return on their RRIF assets instead of the worst-case scenario we have been using. Assuming the Thompsons had adopted the first two enhancements, Table 13.1 shows how much money they would have left in their RRIF at later ages, under two scenarios.

Table 13.1. RRIF assets remaining at age shown (median returns)

	Assets at age 80	Assets at age 90
If they bought an annuity	$313,000	$480,000
If they didn't	$408,000	$557,000

Thus, if investment returns are pretty good, the Thompsons would have more RRIF assets left at age 80 if they *didn't* buy an annuity at 65 than if they did. While the gap narrows a little by age 90, the Thompsons are still better off without the annuity.

The short answer to this revelation is: so what? The whole point to buying an annuity is to have some insurance against both a very long life and very poor investment returns. If neither happens, then naturally you would be better off, since insurance comes at a cost and is supposed to pay off only if the event you are insuring against comes to pass. For instance, you would be better off without home insurance if you never experience a theft, a fire, or a flood but that doesn't mean you don't buy home insurance. You do not know what the future will bring.

Even if you accept the logic for buying an annuity, you might be feeling that the timing isn't right. If that is what is holding you back, I can't blame you. Long-term bond yields, which largely dictate the price of an annuity, are currently below 1 percent. No one predicted this would ever happen because yields have never been this low, not even during the Great Depression. The average yield on long-term bonds from 1936 to 2017 was 5.92 percent. Even in the 1950s, a sedate period known for low interest rates and low inflation, long-term bond yields were almost double what they are today. The lower the yields on bonds, the more expensive it is to buy an annuity.

As a result, you might feel like a chump buying an annuity now only to see yields soar in the years to come. At least, that is the knee-jerk reaction, but let's delve a little further into this question by breaking down the argument into the two main possibilities.

The first possibility is that bond yields will indeed start to climb in the next few years. Maybe the yield will eventually inch up to 3 or 4 percent or even surpass the long-term average of 5.92 percent once again. If this were to happen, the portion of your RRIF that is being invested now in long-term bonds would take a bath. Remember, bond prices *fall* when yields rise. After yields have climbed and the bond portion of your portfolio falls in price 20 or 30 percent, would you really be prepared to sell your bond holdings to buy an annuity?

The second possibility is that bond yields stay extremely low for a long time to come, and possibly go even lower. In my book *The Essential Retirement Guide*, I explained why this was the more likely possibility. I believe that low interest rates are mainly the result of an aging population, not the Great Recession and not COVID-19. Having more people who are over age 50 changes the balance of supply and demand for money, since older people tend to be savers rather than borrowers. Our ratio of older to younger people now is very similar to what it was in Japan 20 years ago. Interest rates there 20 years ago were about the same as ours are today, and their rates have hovered near zero ever since.

Under the "bond yields stay low" rate scenario, bonds may or may not be able to eke out some more capital gains. If they don't, you are looking at a miserable return in the vicinity of 1 or 2 percent a year on your fixed income assets and the cost of an annuity will stay high. If this scenario comes to pass, you will be even less likely to buy an annuity in the future because the cost of the annuity will be as high as it is today, or it might go even higher.

Put the two possibilities together and the conclusion is that "you can't get there from here," meaning if you're not prepared to buy an annuity now, you probably never will be. The only scenario in which you might change your mind is if the following sequence of events happens: (a) you dump all your holdings that you currently have in longer-term bonds and invest in something, stocks perhaps, that might still rise in value even if interest rates rise, (b) interest rates rise, and (c) you take the gains from your investments and use them to buy a less expensive annuity sometime in the future. Frankly, this is a lot to hope for.

In conclusion, you buy an annuity now if you really want protection against the double-whammy of living a very long life and having very poor investment returns. If you don't buy the annuity — and worse comes to worst — it's not the end of the world. For the Thompsons, their income late in their 80s will fall shy of their income target (see Figure 11.1) but only by a little. And remember that Figure 11.1 reflects a 5th-percentile investment scenario. You will probably do better than that. The bottom line is that Enhancement 3 isn't as appealing as it used to be, but for the risk-averse, it is still a keeper.

Buying an Annuity Later

As we have just seen, the case for buying an annuity when interest rates are extremely low is less compelling than when rates are higher. If you put aside today's low interest rates and consider only the question of the optimal age to buy an annuity, we come up with a different answer.

Like a fine wine, annuities get better with age, even if interest rates stay the same. This is because of something called a mortality credit. The mortality credit is there no matter when you buy an annuity, but it is worth a lot more if you buy it at age 75 than at 65. This is because the probability of death at 75 is much greater. I'll provide an example to show how beneficial it can be to buy an annuity in one's 70s instead of at the point of retirement.

> Annuities pay as much income as they do because insurance companies have many annuitants in their pool and each year some of them will die. The insurance company will take this fact into account when they price the annuity. The surviving annuitants benefit by virtue of getting a higher income than if everyone was assumed to die at a ripe old age. This bump in income is the **mortality credit**.

Assume Susan is now 75 and is a widow. She has $100,000 in her RRIF and needs to decide whether to draw an income with that money or purchase an annuity. An annuity with payments guaranteed for five years would provide Susan with annual income of about $8,600. This income would continue to be paid no matter how long she lives.

As for the income from the RRIF, we can already guess that it would underperform the annuity if future investment returns are terrible. But what about if the RRIF produces median returns? In that case, Susan could withdraw about $7,200 a year from her RRIF until age 95 at which point the account would be exhausted. In other words, Susan would (a) get $1,400 a year less income with the RRIF, (b) have the hassle and stress of having to manage the investments or at least be forced to trust someone else to do a good job for her, and (c) would have no protection from the risk of outliving her money if she lives even longer.

In short, the case for buying an annuity gets stronger the older you are when you buy it. If buying an annuity at 75 is better than doing so at age 65, then why not wait until age 80? There are two reasons why I would suggest not putting it off so late. First, the longer you wait, the less likely you are to do it. By age 80, your adult children may very well be helping you manage your financial affairs and they may try to stop you from proceeding with an annuity purchase. Second, the longer you wait, the more exposed you are to a painful market correction happening before the annuity purchase.

ALDAs

The 2019 federal budget introduced **Advanced Life Deferred Annuities** (ALDAs), a vehicle similar to a regular life annuity except that payments start later in life. In fact, they can start as late as age 85, though you give the insurance company the money to pay for it upfront. Your initial reaction might be: "Great, I didn't care for annuities when payments started immediately so why am I going to like them any better when payments start around the time I expect to die?"

So far, the reason most commonly given for buying an ALDA is to reduce the amount you must withdraw from your RRIF. With respect, this is also about the lamest reason. Statistics suggest that most retirees draw down their nest eggs too slowly, not too quickly, so I do not see this as a plus.

The best, and maybe only, reason to consider an ALDA is that you think you might live a long time and want to be sure you have a stream of income over and above your CPP and OAS pensions, just in case your RRIF income runs dry.

When I ran some examples, though, I found that ALDAs were far from the best vehicle to guarantee income in old age. First, an ALDA would exacerbate the problem that was revealed in Figure 12.1. Unless you have savings in the high six figures or more, you might very well have too much income in your 80s and 90s from CPP and OAS alone, at least if you adopted Enhancement 2. Having an ALDA on top of that would exacerbate the situation.

The second problem is that if you do run out of money, it won't happen precisely at age 85. It might happen at 80, in which case you have to endure five years with an income gap.

It turns out that Enhancement 2, deferring CPP to 70, is a better solution than buying an ALDA, at least for couples like Nick and Susan. It does a better job of providing an appropriate amount of income at all ages, including after 85.

A third problem is that annuities in general are not very attractive vehicles while interest rates are so low. ALDAs are even less attractive because the deferral period is longer than for regular annuities, so you are essentially locking in today's low rates for decades.

Still, there are some situations where people can benefit from ALDAs. This is particularly true for high-net-worth individuals, meaning those with asset balances in seven figures. Also likely to benefit from ALDAs are middle-income couples with less CPP pension than Nick and Susan.

Despite all these arguments, if long-term interest rates ever take off, it might be a good idea to revisit ALDAs.

Takeaways

1. If you have a spouse and intend to buy an annuity, it should be a joint and survivor annuity so that payments continue to be made to the surviving spouse.
2. Don't even think about buying an indexed annuity.
3. Buying an annuity is not as effective a strategy as it used to be now that interest rates are so low. That can change, though.
4. You should be earmarking about 20 percent of your tax-sheltered assets for the purchase of an annuity at the point of retirement.
5. It is tempting to wait until you're older, like 75, to buy an annuity and in fact you'll be better off than buying one at 65 *assuming* you don't suffer any investment losses in the interim. This, however, is a dangerous assumption to make.
6. While it is early days, an ALDA does not look like a very effective retirement income vehicle.

CHAPTER 14

Progress Report

Nick and Susan have come a long way since they started on the path to a better decumulation strategy. The "before" picture, as given in Chapter 9, was dismal. Under a worst-case investment scenario, Nick and Susan were shocked to discover just how easy it was to burn through $600,000 of RRIF assets. The money was totally gone by the time Nick was 81 and Susan was 78. They were left with only the income they get from CPP and OAS, which puts them about $30,000 a year short of their income target for the rest of their lives.

It would be easy to conclude that the Thompsons didn't retire with enough money or that they spent it too quickly or invested too recklessly. None of these assertions prove to be true. As the foregoing chapters showed, all they needed was to adopt a better decumulation strategy (and avoid a black swan).

With Enhancement 1 (lower fees), Nick and Susan gave less money to investment managers and kept more of it for themselves. Enhancement 2 transferred much of the investment and longevity risk back to the government by deferring the start of their CPP pensions until age 70.

Enhancement 3 involved the purchase of an annuity with 20 percent of their RRIF balance. This effectively transferred more investment and longevity risks, this time to an insurance company. The result of adopting all three enhancements is shown in Figure 14.1.

Figure 14.1. How the enhancements increase total income

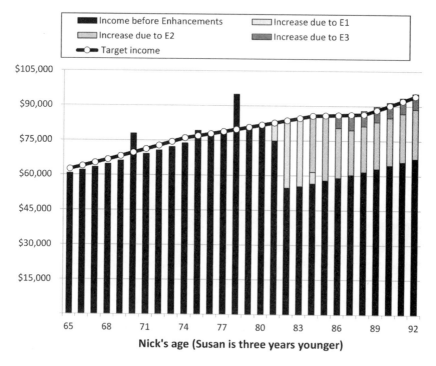

E1 to E3 are Enhancements 1 to 3. Chart assumes they are added sequentially. This assumes 5th-percentile investment returns. Income includes reserve fund.

It is hard to overstate the importance of these actions. From the time that Susan is 79 until her eventual death, which could be well into her 90s, the enhancements give her nearly $30,000 a year in additional income.

It is important to remember that this result is based on the worst-case investment scenario, meaning 5th-percentile investment returns each year. Enhancements 2 and 3 provided insurance against such poor returns and the Thompsons essentially cashed in on that insurance. Enhancement 1 is valuable regardless of the investment scenario.

The Enhancements with Median Returns

To anyone who is really concerned about the consequences of poor returns or simply living a very long time, the previous section should provide ample reason to adopt the enhancements. Nevertheless, it is natural to wonder what would have happened if investment returns had turned out better.

What if the Thompsons had achieved median investment returns instead? Would Enhancements 2 and 3 have hurt them or helped them? To answer this question, I assumed that the Thompsons had median returns and had adopted Enhancement 1 (reduced fees). This became the new base case. After all, reducing fees is a no-brainer. It is a very different type of enhancement compared to Enhancements 2 and 3, which are really a form of insurance.

I also assumed that the Thompsons are counting on median returns so, to be consistent, they may as well set their income target a little higher. Consequently, they start off drawing income of $70,000 from all sources instead of the $62,500 we used in the previous scenarios.

As a result, Nick and Susan reach their new, higher income target every year up until Nick turns 90 (and Susan is 87), and it is only in the following year that the RRIF runs out. This may seem impressive, but it is what you would expect with reduced fees and median returns. If they are still alive at that point, however, they will have an income shortfall of about $35,000 a year in their 90s.

Now let's see what would happen if the Thompsons had adopted Enhancements 2 and 3 when they retired in addition to Enhancement 1. We still have them start out by drawing income at the $70,000 level, the same as the previous scenario. Now, though, there is no income gap until Nick is 95. Equally important, the income gap after age 90 shrinks to only a third of what it would be without Enhancements 2 and 3.

The above analysis should make you feel better about the value of the enhancements, even if you don't think your investment returns will ever be as bad as the 5th-percentile returns we have been assuming.

Takeaways

1. Enhancement 1 is a no-brainer.
2. We already know that Enhancements 2 and 3 should help in a worst-case scenario because both are a form of insurance against poor returns and a long lifespan.
3. What is a bonus is finding that Enhancements 2 and 3 add value even if one achieves median investment returns.

CHAPTER 15

Enhancement 4:
Knowing How Much Income to Draw

As important as the first three enhancements are, they are practically useless if you draw too much or too little income. In the case of the Thompsons, they drew income from all sources of $62,500 in the first year of retirement. This turned out to be just about the right amount for them based on their spending shocks and poor investment returns, though it would have been too much if they hadn't adopted the three enhancements.

What is a little mind-boggling is how a small change in the amount of income being drawn can have such a major impact over the long term. If the Thompsons had started out by drawing just $60,000, they would have had about $160,000 left over at age 95. If their initial draw had been $65,000, they would have run out of money around the time Nick turned 80.

The big question then is how do you establish how much income you can draw from your savings? Equally important, how do you modify the amount you draw over time if your experience is better or worse than you expected? If this is hard to figure out in a simple situation, like that of the Thompsons, how do you cope with a more complex situation, say where you have other sources of income that might vary from year to year, like part-time employment, rental income, investments outside of a tax shelter, money released by downsizing one's home, or a sudden inheritance?

Retirees wrestle with this dilemma all the time. Surveys suggest that most of them resolve the situation by being very conservative in how much they spend. Most people try to avoid touching their capital if they can help it and spend only the investment income. Sure, they would like to spend more, but not if it's going to lead to constant anxiety about a possible future bankruptcy.

This brings us to Enhancement 4. Unlike the previous three enhancements, which all involved ways to stretch one's retirement dollars further, Enhancement 4 is about determining how much income one can draw in retirement. It involves using a retirement income calculator to determine the initial income amount.

Besides determining how much income you can draw in the first year of retirement, Enhancement 4 also involves adjusting that amount in subsequent years as your circumstances change. The idea of actively adjusting your spending — up or down — to reflect your ever-evolving financial situation is essential to a successful decumulation strategy. This is what lies at the heart of Enhancement 4.

Remember that the Thompsons incurred some spending shocks as well as some very poor investment returns. If their luck had been better, Enhancement 4 would have allowed them to draw more income later in retirement. If the spending shocks had been deeper or more frequent, they might have had to draw less. The same sort of adjustments would take place if their investment returns were better or worse than expected.

Enhancement 4 involves using an online retirement income calculator to determine how much income can be drawn from all sources. For this purpose, I created something called PERC, which is short for Personal Enhanced Retirement Calculator. I developed PERC based on the ideas presented in this book, and I employed the services of Morneau Shepell's extensive IT team to make it a reality. PERC is available to the public at no cost and no obligation. Below, I explain how to access PERC and describe in more detail how it works.

Using PERC

To find PERC online, type in PERC.morneaushepell.com in your browser and hit Enter. On the first page you will find a description of PERC, which explains that the user needs to be between ages 50 and 80 to use it. If you are younger than 50, be happy about your relative youth and wait a few years. The other requirement is that the user must be retired or within ten years of retirement. Remember that this book is for people who are close to retirement, not those in mid-career.

The first step is to read the terms of use, click on Agree, and then click on Next. Note that you do not have to provide your email address and, as mentioned earlier, there is no charge to use PERC. My friends at Morneau Shepell have made PERC available to the public, and it is important to me that it be easy to access without the user having to worry about a sales call or ending up on some telemarketer's mailing list.

On the next few screens, you need to enter some basic financial information about yourself. Since you do not divulge your identity anywhere, the information you entered is kept totally confidential. In fact, the system discards your entries after you have finished.

Some of the fields must be completed, and some of them should be kept blank if they do not apply to you. There is a question mark beside most of the boxes where you enter data: click on it and you will see a more detailed explanation on how to answer the given question. In addition, you can refer to Appendix C for more information on how to complete the boxes.

I apologize for the amount of data you have to enter, but it is essential if you want a meaningful answer to the question of how much income you can draw. Once all the data is entered and you press Next one final time, you will see a summary screen that explains that results have been prepared under three scenarios as follows:

Scenario	Description
1	Worst-case (5th-percentile) investment returns and assuming you do not adopt the enhancements
2	Worst-case returns but assuming you do adopt the first three enhancements
3	Same as Scenario 2 except you enjoy median investment returns (which average out to about 5 percent a year)

Scenario 1 is your base case. It assumes your investments do poorly and that you do not adopt any of the enhancements. PERC shows the results under Scenario 1 so that you can see later on how much better you can do by applying the strategies in this book.

Scenario 2 tells you the least amount of income that you should be able to draw safely, even if your investments do very poorly. It applies if you adopt the first three enhancements described in the preceding chapters.

Scenario 3 is more optimistic and assumes median returns on your investments. That is why it shows a higher income level. As long as you use PERC regularly (say annually), you should feel safe drawing income based on this scenario.

To summarize, you should be able to make your savings last a lifetime if your future spending shocks are not too onerous and you keep the total income you draw each year somewhere between the figures produced by Scenario 2 and Scenario 3.

I cannot claim that PERC is the best retirement income calculator out there, but it almost certainly is the only one that explicitly takes the first three enhancements into account. I strongly recommend using PERC on a regular basis.

The Thompsons Use PERC

When the Thompsons input their data into PERC, Scenario 2 shows them that they could draw total income in year 1 of just under $62,900, which is a little more than the $62,500 we have been using in our examples. Under Scenario 3 (median returns), the Thompsons could draw total income of

$70,200. If they don't want to be forced to reduce the amount of income they draw in future years, they might opt to draw an amount closer to $62,900 than to $70,200, but any number in this range is fine as long as they can reel in their spending if things go badly. What is important is that they use PERC regularly to confirm that they are still on the right track.

Enhancement 4 may not seem as dramatic as the other enhancements, but it is essential. Without it, you really cannot know how much income you can safely draw.

Takeaways

1. Without knowing how much income you can safely draw each year, Enhancements 2 and 3 are virtually useless.
2. You can use PERC (an online calculator) to determine how much income you can draw from all sources.
3. There is no charge to use PERC.
4. It is important to revisit PERC on a regular basis, say annually.

CHAPTER 16

Enhancement 5: Have a Backstop

The purpose of the first three enhancements is to reduce risk and to increase the amount of retirement income you can draw safely. Enhancement 4 helps you to keep your spending on track, no matter what happens.

If you adopt all four enhancements, you will probably avoid financial catastrophe during your lifetime. But I can't guarantee it. You might have more spending shocks than average and the amounts involved might be greater. Or you may encounter a black swan event. Finally, you might opt not buy to an annuity at retirement since I gave it a less than ringing endorsement.

With that in mind, let's revisit the Thompsons and introduce a few changes to their situation. We need to do this to be able to illustrate Enhancement 5.

Let's say the Thompsons still adopt Enhancements 1 and 2 but not Enhancement 3 (purchasing an annuity). Here are the other changes we will make:

1. They have the same 5th-percentile returns as before except the return in year 2 is even worse (a loss of 8 percent after fees).

2. They have a fourth spending shock and as a result they draw an extra $20,000 in the year that Nick is 72 and Susan is 69.

3. They don't use PERC to adjust their income draw as their circumstances deteriorate.

The result of making these further changes is shown in Figure 16.1. The Thompsons are short of their target income by about $13,000 when Nick is 81 and Susan is 78. This income gap gradually dwindles in every subsequent year, but they still come up short.

Figure 16.1. The Thompsons come up short

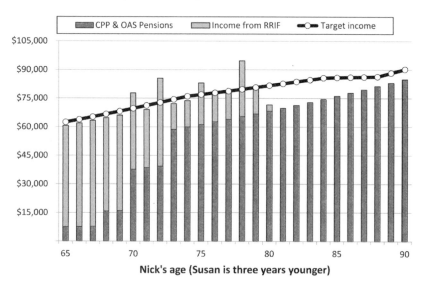

Nick's age (Susan is three years younger)

Same as Figure 13.1 except the Thompsons have one more year of -10% returns, no annuity purchase, and one more spending shock of $20,000.

I need to stress that the changes I made to their situation border on the improbable, but they were necessary to create the income gap. For instance, I assumed they had investment losses of 9.82 percent and 8 percent in their first two years. The median Canadian pension fund has *never* suffered back-to-back losses of this magnitude, at least not since the 1930s, when such records started being kept. The worst return in any two-year period since 1960 was a cumulative loss of 14 percent. (That happened in 1973–1974 by the way, not in 2008–2009 as you might have expected).

The fact the Thompsons kept on spending at the same pace in the face of their money troubles is also unrealistic. This is not what retirees do, especially responsible people like the Thompsons. Even with the extra spending shock and the exceptionally poor investment returns, they could still have muddled through as long as they adjusted their spending downward along the way. The spending adjustments wouldn't even have had to be too onerous. But I had to assume they didn't adjust their spending if I wanted to create an income gap.

The point I am making is that fully implementing Enhancements 1 to 4 makes anyone's decumulation strategy practically bulletproof. Retirees who follow all these steps should have little to worry about. But let's suspend disbelief and assume that the Thompsons fall short of their income target as indicated in Figure 16.1. It is now time to introduce Enhancement 5.

Enhancement 5 is fundamentally different from the others. The first four enhancements might be characterized as "organic," meaning that they're geared to help you make the most of the assets that were specifically meant to be used to produce retirement income. If organic sources of income fall short, however, you need to tap another source.

Enhancement 5 involves making use of your non-financial assets to generate additional income. The most common way to do this is to take out a reverse mortgage on your home (assuming you don't have any Picassos lying around that you could sell instead). I can almost guarantee you won't like to do this, maybe because it doesn't feel "organic."

Even though daytime TV commercials featuring celebrities like Tom Selleck and Kurt Browning tout the virtues of a reverse mortgage, it is hard to find a Canadian who likes this option. For one thing it has the whiff of failure. Taking out a reverse mortgage is a tacit acknowledgement that you failed to manage your finances appropriately. And unless you fully understand how reverse mortgages work, you may have the uneasy feeling that you are getting into a situation beyond your control.

I would be the first to agree that borrowing against your home is not something you should do lightly. But if you have an income gap and the equity in your home is more than enough to close that gap for the rest of your life, you should at least consider it.

Before we get to the mechanics of a reverse mortgage, let's consider Nick and Susan's other options under these straitened circumstances:

- They could resign themselves to living on less money for the rest of their lives.
- They could downsize and move into a smaller home, perhaps in a less expensive community. The savings they realize could be used to boost their income.

Cutting their income by $13,000 is by no means appealing but it is not the end of the world. In the aftermath of the 2008–2009 financial crisis, many retirees had to endure worse. Spending less is also the path of least resistance for many people. Therefore, we cannot rule it out for Nick and Susan.

Downsizing their principal residence is also an option, but that becomes hard to do once the Thompsons are heading into their 80s. No one I know past age 75 has any intention of moving again, except maybe to a retirement home, and that won't happen until their late 80s in most cases.

Even if they do downsize, the Thompsons may not be freeing up as much cash as they had hoped given the myriad costs involved in selling and moving. These costs include real estate commissions, legal fees, repairs and renovations to get the old house ready for sale and the new place ready for moving in, moving costs, sales taxes, and, in most provinces, a land transfer tax.

Let's assume that Nick and Susan are not prepared to slash their budget and leave the middle class behind, nor are they willing to downsize. That leaves them with the option of a reverse mortgage.

Reverse Mortgages Explained

If annuities are the nerds of the retirement planning world, then reverse mortgages would be the black sheep, sort of like that distant cousin who started smoking at 13 and writing graffiti in the school washroom — the cousin your mother warned you to stay away from. A reverse mortgage is perceived negatively because it amounts to a frontal assault on the equity in one's home, an act that is regarded as sacrilegious in this country. We will delve into this widespread perception a little further shortly, but first we'll start with some basic facts.

A reverse mortgage is like a regular mortgage to the extent that you secure a loan from a bank against the equity in your home. There are some important differences, though. With a reverse mortgage, you do not have to make any payments while you or your spouse continue to live in the home. You cannot be forced to move out. You do have to maintain the home, however, including paying property taxes and home insurance premiums on a regular basis.

Another significant difference is in the level of interest rates. With a regular mortgage, the five-year-term fixed rate is roughly 3 percent at the time of writing. The comparable rate for a reverse mortgage (that provides monthly payments) is 5.59 percent. The difference reflects the added risk being assumed by the bank, including the fact that they might very well not see any money coming back to them for decades. The lack of competition in the reverse mortgage market in Canada might be another reason for the big gap in interest rates, as there are only a couple of providers in Canada at this time.

A third difference is the form of payment. With a regular mortgage, the bank gives you the money in a lump sum. The money from a reverse mortgage can also be received in a lump sum, although you can and should opt for a stream of regular monthly payments instead. (The minimum is $500 a month.) Either way, the proceeds are virtually tax-free. We will assume Susan chooses the monthly payments, considering that she is using the money to supplement her income.

You must be 55 or older to qualify for a reverse mortgage and you can keep receiving income payments until the total amount owing reaches 55 percent of the equity in your home. The calculation is based on the equity in the home at the time the mortgage application is made, but the amount could be increased later if an appraisal shows the home has appreciated in value. Also, there are some set-up fees, including legal costs, which might add up to $2,500.

The bank that gives you the money will be first in line to get repaid with interest when you and your spouse have both died or if you move out. No matter how much interest has accumulated, your estate will never have to repay more than the equity in the house, even if the original loan plus accrued interest is greater.

An Example

In Figure 16.1, a shortfall in income first materializes when Nick is 80 and Susan is 77. It grows to about $13,000 in the following year before it starts to shrink a little in each subsequent year. For instance, the shortfall dwindles to $9,000 by the time Nick is 85 and to just $5,000 when he turns 90.

This shortfall is unlikely to come as a complete surprise to Nick and Susan, as they would have been aware for some time that their RRIF assets were running out, so let's assume that they applied for a reverse mortgage when Nick was 80.

They take the income option and elect to receive payments of $833 a month, which is $10,000 a year. This is a little less than the income shortfall in the first few years but since the amount is virtually tax-free it more or less eliminates the entire shortfall on an after-tax basis.

Based on the equity in their home (which is worth $500,000), they have no trouble securing monthly payments to cover the next 15 years. Since this takes them up to the year when Susan turns 92, their money worries effectively disappear.

Of course, this peace of mind comes at a price. The outstanding balance on the reverse mortgage grows to $233,000 by the time Susan is 92 (by which time we will assume she is a widow). The good news is that she doesn't have to pay off the debt as long as she is alive and continues to live in the house. If she does sell, the amount owing is easily covered by the equity in the home as there would still be an estimated $460,000 in home equity remaining. (This assumes a 5.59 percent interest rate on the mortgage and a 2.2 percent annual appreciation rate on the home.)

Pitfalls

Perhaps reverse mortgages are now starting to look a little more respectable than that reprobate cousin. The benefits are reasonably straightforward, but let's delve a little deeper into the possible pitfalls.

First, house prices might fall or at least flatten out. If that happens, there is an outside chance the amount owing will exceed the equity in the home by the time Susan dies or decides to sell. To minimize this risk, it is best not to start a reverse mortgage too early.

Second, buying a reverse mortgage is most appropriate for a homeowner who has no intention of moving again. A move would trigger a repayment with interest, and the total amount paid would be substantially greater than if a regular mortgage had been taken out instead. This is another reason not to start a reverse mortgage too early.

Third, the interest rate for the reverse mortgage might rise over time. The homeowner has little recourse but to accept the higher rates. There are no loan payments to make, but the equity in the home gets drawn down just that much quicker.

Finally, the extra income from a reverse mortgage represents a potential moral hazard. It might tempt some people to indulge in a lifestyle that they may not be able to afford in the long run.

While the risks are real, the potential problems can be minimized by not taking out a reverse mortgage too early in retirement. Even though you can apply as early as 55, I suggest waiting until 75. You face some risk, however, if you wait too long. We have to acknowledge the grim reality that our financial acumen declines with age, even if the confidence we have in our cognitive abilities remains intact. If it were me (and it may be someday), I wouldn't put off a reverse mortgage beyond age 80.

HELOC

A home equity line of credit (HELOC) is another financing option. Because a HELOC involves lower interest rates, it looks more attractive than a reverse mortgage on the surface. Whether it is as viable is a different question.

With a HELOC, you take out only the money you need and the interest rate is set at the prime rate plus 0.5 percent. At the present time, the interest rate would be 4.45 percent. The trouble is that HELOCs are geared to people who have enough income to meet the regular interest payments each month. Given that insufficient retirement income is the reason Susan is considering this option in the first place, this may be a difficult hurdle to overcome.

If the retired homeowner misses an interest payment or if the spouse dies (which reduces income from government pension sources), the lender might call in the loan. This poses just one more hurdle in using a HELOC in lieu of a reverse mortgage.

Clearly, a HELOC is not intended to be a product to help supplement the income of a cash-strapped senior. But let's say that Susan applies for one and manages to persuade the lender to approve it. Consistent with the earlier example, the application is made when Susan is 77, and after it is approved Susan withdraws $860 a month to supplement her retirement income. (The $860 initial payment was chosen to ensure an apples-to-apples comparison with the reverse mortgage.) In each subsequent year, she increases her withdrawal by 4.45 percent. The increases are necessary because the interest payments are growing each year, so the amount borrowed has to cover the increase in payments. This is shown in Table 16.1.

Table 16.1. Interest payments for the HELOC

Susan's age	Amount borrowed in that year	Interest repaid in that year	Net income* for Susan in that year
77	$10,320	$230	$10,090
78	$10,779	$699	$10,080
79	$11,259	$1,189	$10,069
Etc.	Etc.	Etc.	Etc.
90	$18,176	$8,260	$9,916
91	$18,984	$9,087	$9,898

*From the HELOC

By the time Susan is 92, the total amount that she has to repay is $213,700. Under the reverse mortgage, she would have had to repay $233,000. As far as retirement security is concerned, Susan's income situation is virtually the same whether she goes with the HELOC or the reverse mortgage.

It would, therefore, seem that by age 92, Susan is $19,300 ahead by choosing a HELOC over a reverse mortgage. In fact, this gain is illusory. In the first place, Susan would probably not have been able to secure the HELOC given the low income she had after Nick died. Second, this gain is based on there being a gap of 1.14 percent between the interest rate on the reverse mortgage and the HELOC, but who knows how that gap will change over time? Third, Susan might live past 92, and if she had opted for the reverse mortgage, she could stay in her home. With the HELOC, she could be forced to sell her home to pay off the outstanding loan of $213,700; that is, assuming the lender had not already called in the loan and forced her to sell years before.

The other reason why Susan is unlikely to realize that $19,300 advantage is that the HELOC might have been too complicated to set up in the first place, especially considering the constantly increasing payments she would have to receive. Withdrawing a little more each year would have been scary.

In my opinion, there is a place for both products. The HELOC makes more sense if the borrowing is needed only for a short period. It is also preferable if the homeowner plans to move in the short to medium term. All of this, of course, presupposes that the HELOC can even be secured. Otherwise, if you suddenly find yourself near 80 and short of income, you need to be thinking hard about taking out a reverse mortgage.

Takeaways

1. If all else fails, a reverse mortgage can provide much-needed income late in retirement.
2. It is better not to secure a reverse mortgage too early. Wait until age 75 or so but don't wait too long.
3. For a retiree, a reverse mortgage is generally a more viable option than a HELOC.

PART III

Exploring Other Situations

The five enhancements described in Part II put the Thompsons on much more solid financial ground, but their situation was about as simple as it gets — they were 65 and had only RRSP assets. In Part III, we look at how the decumulation strategy handles more complex or challenging conditions, including dying young, retiring early, retiring with a lot more money (or at least many more sources of income), retiring with debt, and retiring single.

CHAPTER 17

What if You Die Early On?

So far, the assumption behind every chart in this book is that Nick and Susan both make it to at least 90. This was a conservative assumption that happened to simplify the analysis. But what if one of them dies at a relatively young age, like in their 70s or even 60s? Do the enhancements still make sense?

While Enhancements 1, 4, and 5 will always be sound, early death puts the other two enhancements into question: deferring CPP (Enhancement 2) and purchasing an annuity (Enhancement 3). Both of these are essentially insurance against living a long time, so you would think you'd be worse off adopting either of them and then dying prematurely. After all, you would have paid for insurance that you didn't use.

In my opinion, this is the wrong way to think about insurance. You buy it because you need protection against a given outcome — in this case, against living a very long time. You cannot know in advance that this outcome will not happen and having the insurance provides you peace of mind in case it does. Nevertheless, you still want to understand the price you are paying for Enhancements 2 and 3 in the event you or your spouse dies early.

What if Nick Dies at 75?

Let's revisit the Thompsons and this time ask what would happen if Nick died just ten years into retirement, at age 75. The probability of a healthy 65-year-old male dying by age 75 is quite low — just 10 percent or so — but clearly it can happen. Death at 75 would trigger the following series of actions:

1. Nick's CPP pension would stop.
2. Susan would get a survivor pension from the Canada Pension Plan in addition to her own CPP retirement pension. (As is described in Appendix D, the calculation of that survivor pension is complicated.)
3. Nick's OAS pension would also stop and there would be no OAS survivor benefit payable to Susan.
4. If they had bought an annuity at the point of retirement, the monthly amount would reduce by one-third* and would be payable to Susan for as long as she lives.
5. Any remaining assets in the RRIF or any other financial vehicle that they had jointly owned would now belong exclusively to Susan.
6. Being single, Susan's income target would be about 30 percent lower than their joint income target when Nick was still alive.

The result of these actions is captured in two charts. Both charts assume they had already reduced their investment fees to 0.6 percent a year (Enhancement 1) since this move was a no-brainer. Figure 17.1 shows the situation if the Thompsons had adopted Enhancement 1 but not Enhancements 2 and 3. In other words, they took CPP early and didn't buy an annuity. They rejected these two enhancements because they were afraid of Nick dying early, which is precisely what happened.

---

* That is because I assume they bought a joint and two-thirds survivor annuity that reduces by a third on either death. Other forms of annuity exist.

As the chart shows, the RRIF assets dry up ten years after Nick's death, when Susan is 82. From age 83 on, Susan's total income is short of even her reduced income target by a whopping $26,000 a year.

Figure 17.1. Nick dies early; only Enhancement 1 was adopted

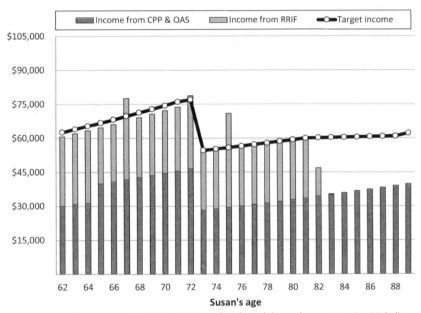

The Thompsons start their CPP immediately and do not buy an annuity. Nick dies at 75 (when Susan is 72). The RRIF runs out a little sooner, but the income gap is smaller.

Figure 17.2 shows what would have happened if the Thompsons had adopted Enhancements 2 and 3 in addition to Enhancement 1. At first blush, this chart might seem to confirm that Enhancements 2 and 3 are poor choices if one of them dies early. Their RRIF assets run out when Susan is just 79, which is almost four years sooner than in the first scenario.

Figure 17.2. Nick dies early; Enhancements 1 to 3 are in place

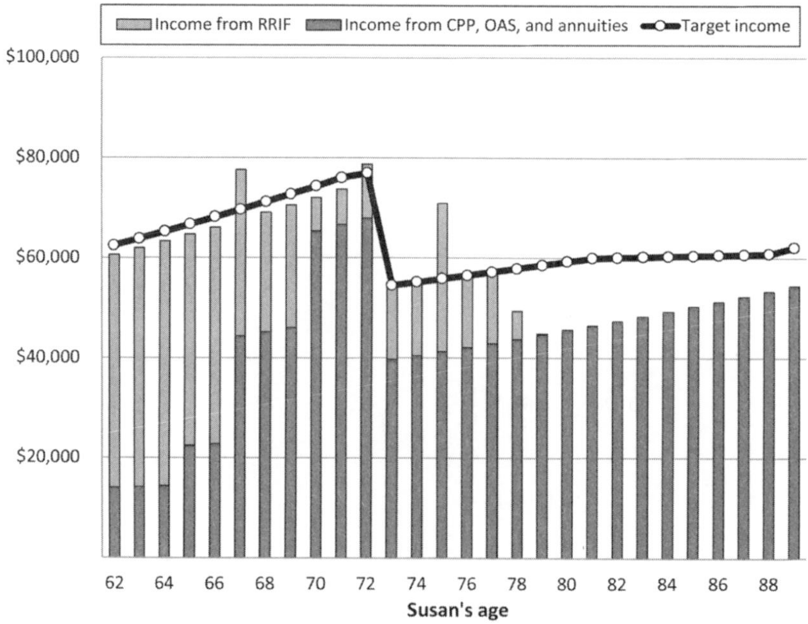

In this scenario, the Thompsons buy an annuity when Nick is 65 and both start CPP at 70. Income target drops by 30% when Nick dies.

If you take a closer look at the two charts, however, you will find that Enhancements 2 and 3 are not so bad after all, even if Nick dies early. Notice that Susan's income gap is much smaller as a result of having adopted Enhancements 2 and 3. That is because Susan has her annuity as well as a much bigger CPP pension. The income gap when Susan is age 79 is $14,000 versus $26,000 without extra enhancements; after that, it shrinks to just $7,000 a year by the time Susan is 88.

If we make the comparison a little more scientific, note that the sum of all the annual income gaps from the time Susan is 81 until she is 90 is $132,000 if they reject the two enhancements versus $113,000 if they adopt them.

That might not seem like much of an improvement, but remember that we shouldn't have expected any improvement at all. Enhancements 2 and 3 are great if Nick and Susan both live until 90, but they weren't expected to help if one of them dies young. And yet they do help, at least a little. Essentially, it means there is little or no cost to the insurance that Enhancements 2 and 3 were meant to provide.

To be sure, there is still a shortfall, but let's not forget Enhancement 4. Much of the income gap, and possibly all of it, could have been avoided if Susan had used Enhancement 4 to determine how much income she could draw each year after Nick's death.

A Surprise if Nick Dies at 68

Now let's consider an even more extreme situation. What if Nick had died at 68? If he had previously decided to defer his CPP pension until 70, such an early death means he would never collect a cent from CPP. Surely Enhancement 2 fails miserably in this case?

It turns out that even if Nick dies at 68, deferring CPP to 70 would still be the best option for Susan's long-term financial well-being. How can this be?

For one thing, some of Nick's CPP pension does get paid, only not to Nick. About 60 percent of it is paid as a survivor benefit to Susan until she turns 70 and starts to collect her own CPP pension. After that, the survivor benefit is reduced so that Susan's own retirement pension plus the survivor benefit do not exceed the maximum CPP pension payable to any one individual. In spite of this reduction at 70, Susan is still *much* better off than if she and Nick had elected to start their CPP early. When you add up all of Susan's annual income gaps from ages 81 to 90, the total shortfall is just $36,000 if the Thompsons had adopted Enhancements 2 and 3 versus $115,000 if they didn't.

Takeaways

1. Enhancements 2 and 3 are essentially insurance against living a very long life.
2. Even if one spouse dies young, the surviving spouse is still financially better off if the couple had adopted Enhancements 2 and 3 at the point of retirement.

CHAPTER 18

Super-Savers and YOLOs

The Thompsons are like most middle-income Canadian couples on the verge of retirement, which is why I called them mainstream retirees. They will rely heavily on their CPP and OAS pensions, but they will very much need the money from their RRSPs and investment vehicles to maintain a comfortable lifestyle after retirement. The Thompsons want those savings to generate as much income as possible but not at the risk of running out. As for bequests, it would be nice to be able to leave a little money to their loved ones but that isn't their highest priority.

Described below are two other types of retirees.

Super-Savers

Some retirees are more cautious than others. When they were still working, the cautious ones socked away a little more for retirement than average, and after they retire, they will spend less than mainstream retirees with similar assets. I call these people Super-Savers.

If you have a Super-Saver living in your neighbourhood, you wouldn't be surprised to find that they:

- keep a ten-year-old Buick in their garage,
- have an even older TV set in their living room, probably 32-inch,
- seldom dine out except at Swiss Chalet,
- haven't bought furniture since the Mulroney era,
- always turn off the lights when they leave a room,
- save their drugstore shopping for seniors' day, and
- vacation in Florida, not in Aruba.

Super-Savers generally try extra hard not to touch their capital, and in good years, their assets continue to rise. Their children are sure to inherit most of their money some day and will probably feel a little guilty about spending it.

Academics used to attribute the spending habits of Super-Savers to memories of the Great Depression, but there are still many Super-Savers out there and always will be. There are a variety of reasons why Super-Savers are the way they are. Some do not fully understand how much they can afford to spend and err on the side of caution. Some may know they can probably spend more but have lower risk tolerance than most people. And finally, some Super-Savers might feel it is just plain wrong to be spending so much on themselves after a lifetime of frugality; they are more comfortable maintaining a modest lifestyle.

There is a special category of Super-Savers that I will call the Cleavers — not the butcher-knife variety but rather the TV family from the iconic 1950s show *Leave It to Beaver*. Ward and June Cleaver would have been mainstream retirees were it not for the "Beaver" (son Theodore). The Beaver got in trouble in virtually every episode as a result of exhibiting consistently poor judgment. A real-life Beaver would find it difficult making his way through life on his own, which is why parents like the Cleavers figure they will need to continue providing financial support for their children, possibly even beyond the grave. Extensive anecdotal evidence suggests that couples who fit this description are surprisingly common. Many of my friends and acquaintances around retirement age are quietly making provisions for a grown-up child who, they fear, will be unable to cope once they are gone.

Because they have a special need to help out a grown-up child, the Cleavers will have spending habits that are similar to other Super-Savers. The Cleavers just have a more specific reason for spending less.

Super-Savers are almost certain to end their lives with a significant amount of unspent capital and this might well be their intent. For purposes of calculating the income they can draw from their assets, we can treat Super-Savers the same as mainstreamers who hold back a greater portion of their assets if they happen to live into their 90s.

Strategy for Super-Savers

Super-Savers will have no trouble implementing Enhancement 1 (reducing fees) since it means paying less for investment management. They will be very reluctant to embrace Enhancement 2, however. Deferring their CPP pension forces them to spend down their savings more quickly, which pains them more than it does the average mainstream retiree. They will probably have the same qualms about Enhancement 3; buying an annuity does not reduce their overall retirement wealth but it does make some of it — the portion used to buy an annuity — practically invisible.

Super-Savers will be happy to use PERC (Enhancement 4) but will draw income at the low end of what the calculator says they can draw safely, or maybe even less than that. As for Enhancement 5 (a reverse mortgage), they will almost certainly never need to go there, which is just as well since they would hate the idea of tapping into their home equity late in life.

I don't expect Super-Savers to abandon their habits and suddenly start spending more, but I would still strongly encourage them to adopt the first four enhancements. The one thing they might do differently than Mainstreamers is to hold back a portion of their assets when entering data into PERC. For instance, if they had $500,000 in a RRIF and another $100,000 in stocks or GICs outside of any tax-sheltered vehicle, they might ignore the latter amount when trying to figure out how much income they can draw.

YOLOs

At the other end of the spectrum are the YOLOs, as in "you only live once." YOLOs will want to spend more extravagantly in their early retirement years, even if it dims their longer-term prospects a little. Some people prefer immediate gratification and are YOLOs by nature. Others become YOLOs because they think their life expectancy is shorter than normal and want to enjoy life while they can. Still others expect a normal lifespan but are more focused on ensuring they make the most of their disability-free life expectancy, which can be a lot shorter than total life expectancy. (They might have gotten that idea from my last book.) YOLOs do not want to be destitute in old age, but their bigger fear is finding themselves at the end of their lives with a great deal of unspent wealth.

YOLOs will not have a problem adopting Enhancement 1. It just gives them that much more money to spend on themselves. They should also be less reluctant than most retirees about adopting Enhancement 2 since they have less resistance in general to drawing down their savings.

They won't be especially keen about Enhancement 3, though, since it pushes some of their wealth into their extreme old age. As for Enhancement 4, they will want to be spending at the top end of the range suggested by PERC, which should be fine, provided they use PERC regularly. Finally, they are more likely than other Canadians to consider a reverse mortgage (Enhancement 5), not only by their nature but because they are more likely to need it.

In my experience, YOLOs are rare in Canada, which is a little strange since their philosophy seems perfectly rational.

Other Types

You might be wondering where the worrywart fits into this catalogue of retiree types. I don't really see retirees who worry a lot about their financial situation as a separate type since I have witnessed a spectrum of worry within each of the main types described above.

Some people will fret more than others by nature, whether they have reason to do so or not. My late father had accumulated considerable wealth in his lifetime, thanks to some shrewd investments in real estate in the 1960s, and yet he still had lingering concerns in his late 80s that his money would run out. Nothing could have been further from the truth, though. He lived very frugally to the end and my best guess is that he would have had enough money to last him and my mother a couple of centuries. To be sure, he was an extreme case. My father was a classic Super-Saver, and I doubt he ever regretted not spending more money when he could have. Perhaps he rests easier knowing his grandchildren and even his great-grandchildren will benefit from the legacy that his personal frugality made possible.

Ultimately, most anxiety in retirement stems from uncertainty. If you had low but certain income, you might be a little miserable (or not) but you wouldn't be particularly anxious. Surveys show that retirees whose income is variable (because they are living off their savings and are exposed to risk) are more likely to remain in a state of anxiety long after they retire. This response is totally rational and largely explains why I wrote this book — to offer a decumulation strategy that will wring out much of the variability and lessen that anxiety.

Perhaps the luckiest retirees from a financial perspective are those who have ample pensions from defined benefit (DB) pension plans. They tend to worry less about finances in retirement and spend more freely. Unfortunately, DB plans are dying out (except in the public sector) because of the financial strain they place on employers. Fewer than 10 percent of all workers in the private sector are still members of DB plans, and this percentage will keep dwindling, as most DB plans are now closed to new members.

The most important result that comes from a smart decumulation strategy is the ability to produce a stream of income that is stable and predictable, almost as if it came from a DB plan.

Takeaway

1. There are at least two other types of retirees, Super-Savers and YOLOs. The decumulation strategy presented in Part II works for them as well, but with some tweaks.

CHAPTER 19

How Early Retirement Changes Everything

If Nick and Susan wanted to retire earlier, their financial situation becomes more challenging. For instance, imagine they were age 60 and 57 at the point of retirement, instead of 65 and 62. Let's assume they had the same earnings and CPP contribution history between 18 and 60 as before. Let's also assume that they somehow still managed to save $600,000 in their RRSPs, though now they did it five years sooner. In that case, here is what they can expect:

1. **Smaller CPP pension**: Until now, I have assumed that Nick's CPP pension at 65 would be 90 percent of the maximum payable at 65. If he waited until 70 to collect his CPP, it would be 90 percent of the maximum payable at age 70. The reason the 90 percent figure doesn't change is because you don't have to count the years between ages 65 and 70 in the CPP calculation.

   The situation is quite different at age 60. If he had earned 90 percent of the maximum pension payable at 60 but elected to wait until age 65 or older to start payments, Nick would have to include the years between ages 60 and 65 in the CPP calculation. If Nick had no employment earnings in those five years, his pension at 65 or older would drop from 90 percent of the maximum CPP pension down to 79 percent.

The same principle applies to Susan. All the calculations up until now have assumed that she had made enough CPP contributions to collect 70 percent of the maximum CPP pension. If she was entitled to 70 percent of the maximum at age 60 and waits until 65 or later to collect it, her entitlement would drop to just 59 percent of the maximum.

The dilution in their CPP pensions caused by waiting to collect will no doubt be distressing, but the question is whether it is reason enough to start collecting CPP immediately. The short answer is no. I explain why later in this chapter.

2. **More assets needed to produce the right income curve**: If Nick and Susan retire at age 60 with $600,000, they'll find that they don't have enough money to put Enhancement 2 fully into effect. If they deferred their CPP pension until 70, they wouldn't have enough income from other sources before 70 and, at the same time, their income would end up being substantially above the target income curve in their later years. We had already uncovered the problems with this sort of result back in Chapter 12, when we analyzed how much money was needed to implement Enhancement 2. Based on retirement at age 60 with $600,000 (and assuming the same spending shocks as before), I calculate that the ideal age to start CPP is 67.

3. **Less overall income**: It is obvious that if you stretch the same amount of assets over five more years of retirement, your annual income inevitably shrinks. You might be surprised, though, by just how much. At ages 60 and 57, the Thompsons' $600,000 in assets produces only $48,000 in annual income in year 1 of retirement versus the $62,500 we determined earlier if they were five years older with the

same assets. (This is all based on the worst-case investment scenario, the three spending shocks, and the assumption they adopted the first three enhancements.) If they still wanted $62,500 in income in the first year of early retirement, they would need about $1,300,000 in RRIF assets.

4. **Enhancements 1 and 2 become even more important**: In previous chapters, we established how valuable the first three enhancements can be for a couple who are retiring close to age 65. This is just as true in the case of a couple who are retiring at a younger age. Without the enhancements, the Thompsons can afford to draw income of only $42,500 in year 1 (when Nick is 60) versus nearly $48,000 with the enhancements.

5. **But Enhancement 3 is not so important**: Buying an annuity is a hedging strategy that is more effective at older ages. In the case of the Thompsons on early retirement, they derive almost the same result by adopting only the first two enhancements and not bothering with the annuity.

6. **You can't receive your OAS pension yet**: The government lets you start your CPP pension as early as age 60 but not OAS pension. You must be 65 to receive OAS. Early retirees will have to fill the income gap that this creates by drawing more income from other sources, such as their RRIF.

7. **The tax situation is less favourable before 65**: Retirees generally find that they pay much less income tax than when they were working. There are many reasons for this, and if you are considering early retirement, it is important to know that some of those reasons do not apply until you reach age 65. For instance, age 65 is when you are first eligible for the age amount tax credit. It is also when you can start to split income with your spouse. Hence, if you retire early, expect to pay a little more income tax for a few years.

What about CPP Dilution?

Above, I explained that if Nick starts his CPP pension at 60, he will receive 90 percent of the maximum amount payable at that age. If he stops working at 60 and waits until 65, his CPP entitlement is only 79 percent of the maximum. His entitlement is diluted by having five more years of no CPP contributions.

It is this dilution in the CPP benefit that makes most early retirees want to start collecting their CPP earlier rather than later. But let's face it: they would have wanted to collect it earlier anyway. I have already shown that the Thompsons are better off deferring their CPP to at least age 67 and maybe age 70 rather than taking it at 60. The question readers might ask is: how is this possible given the dilution factor?

The reason it is still better to defer your CPP pension to 65 or older is that you avoid the punitive early retirement reduction imposed by the Canada Pension Plan rules. Your CPP benefit is reduced by 7.2 percent for each year that CPP starts before age 65. If you were age 60 when you started to collect CPP, your CPP benefit would be reduced by 36 percent so, yes, you might be getting 90 percent of the maximum payable at 60, but that maximum is 36 percent less than it would be at age 65. In other words, the dilution factor described earlier is more than offset by the early retirement reduction factor.

Takeaways

1. Retiring early is much more of a challenge than waiting until age 65. Not only do your savings produce much less income, you pay more in income tax.
2. If you retire early, it takes much more assets to put Enhancement 2 into effect.
3. If you stop working before age 65, you are still better off waiting until 65 or later to collect CPP (assuming you have enough other assets), in spite of the dilution caused by having a few more years of no CPP contributions.

CHAPTER 20

Not Yet Ready to Retire?

Originally, this book was targeted exclusively at people who were either already retired or on the verge of retirement. In other words, it was meant for people whose saving days were over. Their nest egg wasn't going to grow any bigger and it was just a matter of how much income they could safely squeeze out of it.

To my surprise, almost no one I know who asked for my help fell into my original target audience. While they were all over 50, they were still a few years away from pulling the trigger on retirement. What makes their situation different from immediate retirees is that they wanted to know what steps they could take to improve their situation while they still had employment income. It is for readers like them that I added this chapter.

It is also why I changed the retirement income calculator (PERC) to handle ongoing employment income and to reflect additional contributions to an RRSP, TFSA, or other tax-assisted retirement vehicle. PERC allows people who are still actively employed to predict their future retirement income, provided that retirement occurs within the next ten years.

Anyone who is within ten years of retirement who applies the ideas described in Part II should be able to avoid nasty financial surprises after they retire. To this end, they should make it a priority to pay off their mortgage and any other debt. In addition, they might want to pad their RRSP and TFSA balances.

The key is to use PERC to figure out in advance how much money you will have accumulated by your projected retirement date and the income it can produce. If you don't like the answer, then you rerun the forecast assuming you save more in your remaining working years or push back your retirement age. This could be an iterative process.

An example will help to illustrate how this might work. Let's assume that Anil and Rhea are hoping to retire in three years' time. Their current financial situation is set out in the table below.

Table 20.1. Data on Anil and Rhea (Scenario 1)

	Anil	Rhea
Current age	57	54
CPP pension (as % of maximum)	80%	70%
Current RRSP balance	$300,000	$200,000
Current TFSA balance	$60,000	$40,000
Outstanding mortgage balance	$50,000	Nil
Years until mortgage is paid off	3	NA
Employment income (gross)	$80,000	$40,000
Planned RRSP contribution (annual)	$5,000	$3,000
Planned TFSA contribution (annual)	$6,000	$6,000

After entering all this information into PERC, Figure 20.1 shows what they can expect if they experience worst-case investment returns and implement Enhancements 1 to 3.

The result is somewhat mixed. On the positive side, they can look forward to annual income of about $48,000 in their first year of retirement (when Anil is 60 and Rhea is 57). This income will rise annually until their 90s based on the income growth curve we established in Chapter 5.

The negatives, however, outweigh the positives. Their income in the first year of retirement is lower than it was in their last three years of work,

Figure 20.1. If they retire in three years (Scenario 1)

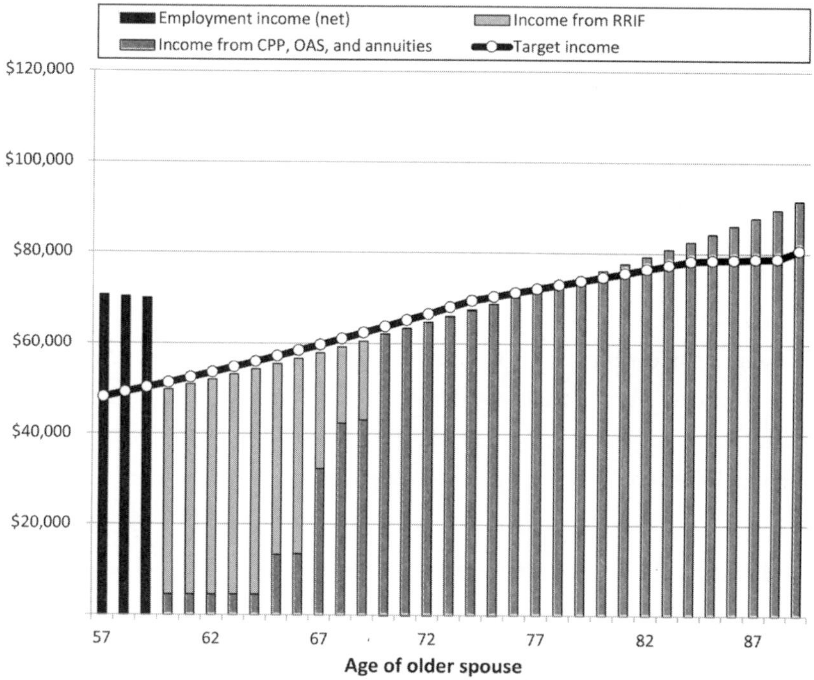

Legend:
- Employment income (net)
- Income from CPP, OAS, and annuities
- Income from RRIF
- Target income

(y-axis: $20,000 to $120,000; x-axis: Age of older spouse, 57 to 87)

Assumes 5th-percentile returns. Mortgage paid off by retirement. Modest RRSP contributions until retirement.

even when we deduct RRSP and TFSA contributions as well as mortgage payments from employment income. If they really need to have that much disposable income in their last three working years, then they are in for a rude shock when they retire.

Second, they don't have quite enough assets in their RRIFs and TFSAs to follow the income target curve in all years. By the time they are in their 80s, they are getting too much income. This is why I assume they start CPP at age 67 instead of 70, an idea that I described in Chapter 12. You need a lot more assets to fully implement Enhancement 2 (deferring CPP) if you retire much earlier than 65.

By the way, the above chart and projections assume that Rhea and Anil transfer their RRSP monies into an RRIF early but this was just to keep the example simple. In a real-life situation, they would probably just make annual withdrawals from their RRSP and save the RRIF buying until much later.

Retiring in Five Years Instead of Three

In the second scenario, Anil and Rhea resign themselves to working two extra years, which means retiring when Anil is 62 and Rhea is 59. This gives them more time to build up their RRSPs and TFSAs. They are now contributing $14,000 and $7,000 to their RRSPs and are doing so for five more years instead of three. They are still contributing $6,000 a year to their TFSAs.

Later retirement also makes it easier to pay off the balance on their mortgage, since they can now spread the payments over five years. The other positive effect is that later retirement boosts their CPP entitlement by another 5 percent each, since they each have two more years of CPP contributions. The result of these changes is shown in Figure 20.2.

Figure 20.2. Save more and retire in five years (Scenario 2)

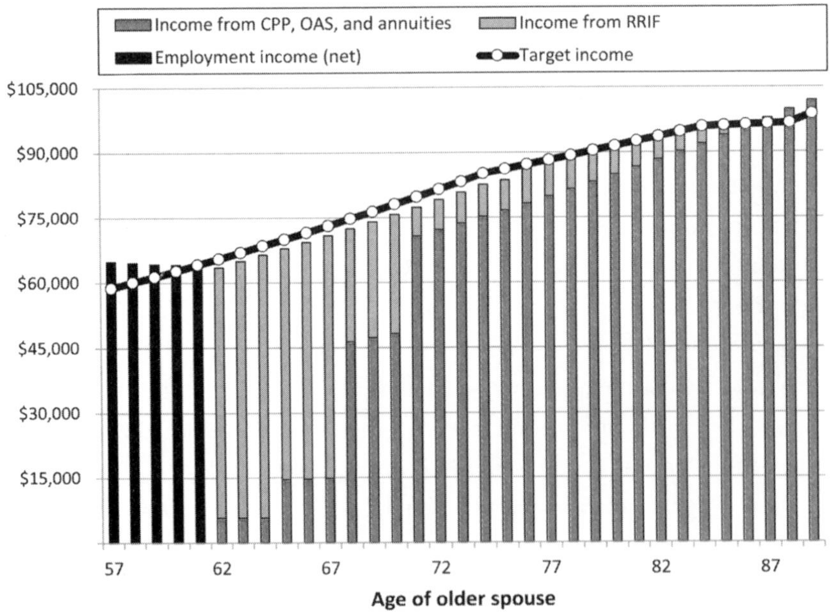

Still 5th-percentile investment returns. Retirement now is in five years' time, and they contribute $14,000 and $7,000 a year to RRSPs. CPP deferred until 68. Income is about $12,000 a year higher.

Retiring under Scenario 2 looks a lot more promising than under Scenario 1. Their income from all sources in their first year of retirement (when Anil is 62 and Rhea is 59) is over $65,000 now, versus $48,000 under Scenario 1. Also, the problem of not being able to stay on the ideal income target curve is almost eliminated (they start CPP at 68 instead of 67).

Please keep in mind that these calculations assume worst-case investment returns. If they can obtain median investment returns instead, the amount of income in their first year of retirement under Scenario 2 soars to $87,000. While this would be great, they shouldn't count on it. Anil and Rhea shouldn't base their retirement decisions on the hope of median returns that might not materialize.

Another question is whether working two more years to improve their finances in retirement is worth it. I can't answer that question as the answer will depend on factors that are not easily quantified, such as health and the stress involved in their working environment. Moreover, their plans might change depending on how their investments perform. If their returns are better than expected, they might be able to move up their retirement date a little. What is important is that they can use PERC to model all of this, well in advance of retirement.

Takeaway

1. PERC can be a useful tool to tweak your retirement planning if you still plan to work a few more years.

CHAPTER 21

Complex Situations

The financial situation of the Thompsons was about as simple as it gets. Their only non-government source of retirement income was their RRSP and they had no debt.

In this chapter, we will look at a more complicated situation that will be closer to reality for many retirees. It will feature another couple who are on the verge of retirement, Steve and Cathy Wong. Steve (64) and Cathy (60) operated a successful sporting goods business, which they are now winding down. Here are the details on their financial holdings:

- They have $350,000 in RRSPs and another $90,000 in TFSAs between the two of them.
- They have $70,000 in stocks and bonds in a self-directed account outside of their RRSPs and TFSAs. The money will be subject to an average income tax rate of 10 percent when they sell the securities.*

---

* It is low because they paid income tax previously on much of it and the rest will be taxed as a capital gain rather than ordinary income.

- They own a condominium worth $450,000 that they rent out. The gross annual amount they are collecting from the tenant is $18,000 but from this amount they deduct property taxes, condo maintenance fees, repairs and insurance, which leaves them with net rental income of $8,000 a year. There is a $100,000 balance on the mortgage on the condo on which they are making monthly payments of $1,000 for another ten years. As a result, their net annual cash flow from the condo is negative $4,000.
- Their home is worth $900,000, but they took out a home equity line of credit a few years back and still owe $75,000. Their plan is to repay it over three years at $27,500 a year, including interest.
- Steve plans to work part-time for another three years and will pull in $30,000 a year. He will contribute $6,000 to his TFSA each year.
- Steve is entitled to 79 percent of the maximum CPP payable at 64, if he starts payments now, versus 78 percent if he starts CPP at 65 or later.
- If Cathy starts CPP immediately, she gets 78 percent of the maximum payable at 60. If she starts it at 65 or later, only 67 percent of the maximum CPP is payable.
- They set up a reserve for spending shocks and contribute 3 percent of income to it each year until Steve is 75.

The challenge is to turn this hodgepodge of assets, income, and debts into a steady stream of income over their lifetime. Fortunately, it is just a matter of entering all the data into PERC, which will do the work for us. We will look at several scenarios.

In Scenario 1, Steve and Cathy hold onto their rental property for another ten years and then sell it for $470,000, which represents a $20,000 appreciation in value from the current price. After we net out transaction costs and a small amount of capital gains tax, they clear about $440,000. In addition, they reduce their investment fees on their RRSPs and TFSAs (Enhancement 1) but take a pass on Enhancements 2 and 3. This is all depicted in Figure 21.1.

Figure 21.1. The Wongs reject Enhancements 2 and 3

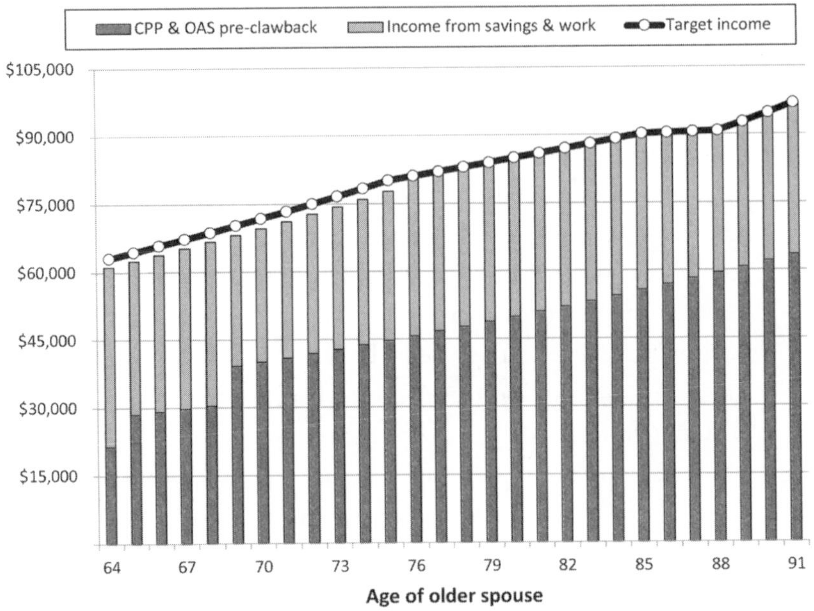

Legend: CPP & OAS pre-clawback | Income from savings & work | Target income

X-axis: Age of older spouse (64, 67, 70, 73, 76, 79, 82, 85, 88, 91)

Y-axis: $15,000 to $105,000

Steve and Cathy adopt Enhancement 1 but not 2 and 3. They incur 5th percentile returns. Income from savings & work includes the condo and is net of debt repayment.

In the above scenario, the Wongs successfully manage to turn some very lumpy assets into a smooth income stream. The only problem is that they are taking on a fair amount of risk to do so. What if they can't sell their condo in ten years' time for anywhere close to $470,000? What if they lose their tenant and take awhile finding another (and possibly incur major renovation expenses on the condo to attract a new tenant)?

Let's park the condo problem for a moment and assume that the only change the Wongs make is to adopt Enhancements 2 and 3. (They wait until Steve is 67 to buy the annuity since Steve will still be working part-time up until then.) The result is shown in Figure 21.2.

While Enhancements 2 and 3 usually work like a charm, they fail here. The Wongs face a severe cash flow shortage eight years into retirement. The cause is not insufficient wealth but rather not enough liquidity. Holding onto the condo for ten years is not compatible with adopting Enhancements 2 and 3, at least not in this case. In general, holding

Figure 21.2. The Wongs adopt Enhancements 2 and 3

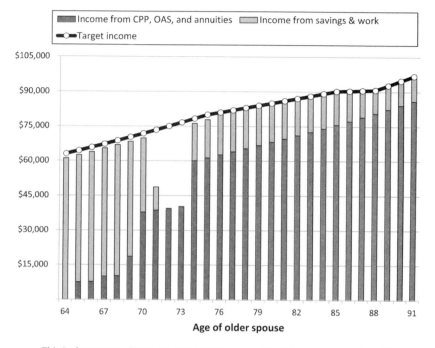

This is the same as Figure 21.1 except they now adopt Enhancements 2 and 3. This creates a cash flow problem in their early 70s because they haven't sold the condo yet.

onto real estate or other illiquid investments that produce minimal net income can make it difficult or impossible to achieve a smooth income stream.

In this case, the Wongs can reduce the risk of being a landlord and take advantage of Enhancements 2 and 3 by doing one thing: they sell their condo just six years into retirement instead of ten. This solves both their cash flow problems and reduces risk, since they are no longer landlords after the sale. They meet their income target each year (not illustrated) and have a significant amount of savings remaining as they enter their 90s.

This is true even though the net proceeds on selling the condo (I am assuming $352,000) are less after six years than after ten because there is still a small mortgage remaining and the property hasn't appreciated as much in value.

Takeaways

1. PERC is useful in taking an assortment of "lumpy" assets from many sources and turning them into a smooth income stream.
2. If you want to create a smooth income stream, you may have to sell off illiquid assets, such as an investment property, sooner than you otherwise would.

CHAPTER 22

High-Net-Worth Couples

To many Canadians, the Thompsons qualify as a high-net-worth couple on the strength of their $600,000 in investable retirement assets. To investment managers who cater to high-net-worth individuals, the investable amount would need to be significantly greater than that to get them interested in you as a client.

It is time to introduce the Clarkes. Joel and Colleen Clarke have $3 million in investable assets as well as a paid-off house worth over $1 million.

Not all the Clarkes' $3 million in assets is contained within tax-sheltered vehicles. The dollar limits imposed by the government on tax-deductible contributions make it difficult to accumulate that much wealth in tax-sheltered arrangements unless you're a high-level civil servant. In the case of the Clarkes, they hold some of their money in non-tax-sheltered assets (NTS assets).

The key components of their holdings are given in Table 22.1.

I will assume that the Clarkes incur four spending shocks between the time Joel is 67 and 78 and that the shocks total $110,000. This is more than what the Thompsons had to endure, but we should expect that the size of shocks will grow in line with one's net worth. (If the amounts stayed small, they wouldn't really be shocks.) Given their sizeable financial resources, we will assume that the Clarkes do not bother to set up a reserve fund to cover the spending shocks.

Table 22.1. Data on Joel and Colleen

Joel's and Colleen's ages	65 and 62
Savings in RRIFs	$2,000,000
Savings in TFSAs	$200,000
Savings that are not tax-sheltered	$800,000
Joel's estimated CPP (as a % of maximum)	100%
Colleen's estimated CPP (as a % of maximum)	75%
Annual investment fees before Enhancement 1	1.80%

The first thing we will calculate is how long their money will last if they draw total income of $140,000 in year 1 plus inflationary increases in future years. They use PERC (Enhancement 4) to determine this number. In the first scenario, the Clarkes do not adopt any of the enhancements, and as in most of the projections so far, they incur 5th-percentile investment returns. The result is shown in Figure 22.1.

The Clarkes start to run short of money when Joel is 86 and Colleen is 83. This was bad enough in the case of the Thompsons but even worse for the Clarkes, if only because the Clarkes have much higher income expectations. Living off just their CPP and OAS income isn't really an option for them.

Next, we will add Enhancement 1. Given the size of their portfolio, the Clarkes can probably get their fees down to just 0.5 percent, but we will continue to assume that Enhancement 1 reduces their fees to 0.6 percent, the same as it did for the Thompsons. While not illustrated here, lowering fees makes a significant difference. Their money lasts five years longer than in the previous scenario. On the other hand, lower fees alone do not ensure total security, as they have no assets left to generate income by the time Joel is 91 and Colleen is 88.

Figure 22.1. Income projection before any enhancements

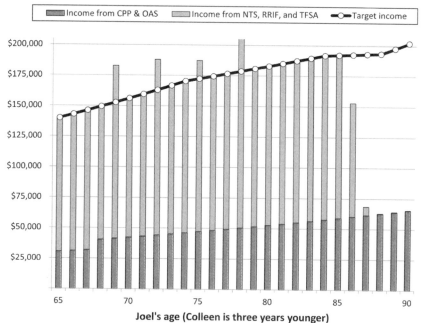

Joel's age (Colleen is three years younger)

5th-percentile investment returns. Four spending shocks totaling $110,000. Investment fees of 1.8%. Asset mix is 50-50.

We then add in Enhancement 2, deferring CPP to 70. So long as one of them lives to a ripe old age, this further change helps significantly. Their money now lasts until Joel is 95.

Finally, we test to see whether Enhancement 3 (buying an annuity) helps much. The result is that they now have $157,000 in assets remaining at age 95 versus almost none after we added Enhancement 2. In addition, the amount of secure income — from CPP, OAS, and an annuity — is now higher, which would be important in the unlikely event that their investments do even more poorly than the 5th-percentile returns we have been assuming.

This last scenario is a good outcome, but not one that means very much to the Clarkes unless one of them lives beyond 95. Moreover, it will not help at all if their investment returns are closer to the median rather than the 5th percentile.

By the way, if the Clarkes had bought an annuity with 30 percent of their RRIF assets instead of 20 percent, the amount of money they would still have left at age 95 more than doubles to $323,000. Moreover, they would have a higher level of secure income in each year leading up to age 95. Depending on how risk-averse the Clarkes are, this higher allocation to annuities might look quite attractive.

Because of the Clarkes' greater financial resources, another option is open to them that wasn't readily available to the Thompsons. Not only should they defer their CPP to age 70, they should defer their OAS pensions to 70 as well. You will recall that deferring OAS by five years increases the amount of pension payable by 36 percent. In the case of middle-income couples like the Thompsons, I didn't endorse this strategy because it accelerates the drawdown of savings beyond the point at which most people would feel comfortable. This shouldn't be an issue for the Clarkes.

By deferring OAS to 70, the Clarkes can buy a little extra peace of mind. In the event of worst-case investment returns, they end up having another $100,000 in assets remaining when Joel is 95. They also have a higher level of secure income in each year up to that age.

The most important insight we can get from these projections is that Enhancement 1 (reduced fees) is by far the most important of the three enhancements in the case of high-net-worth individuals.

Deferring CPP to 70 is also worthwhile, as it provides much better income security in their late 80s and does so at no cost. This enhancement would be less valuable if the Clarkes still had employment income beyond age 65. In that case, they might be better off starting their CPP pensions at 65. (See Appendix D for more on this point.)

As for purchasing an annuity, it makes a difference only in the most extreme situations (such as when investment returns are especially poor or lifespans are unusually long) and even then, the difference is not that great. On the other hand, buying the annuity is never a terrible idea.

Finally, I note that at higher-income levels, the **OAS clawback** might also come into play and could affect the implementation of the enhancements. Its impact is marginal, however, even in the case of Joel and Colleen. One needs very high income for the clawback to be much of a factor, so we will ignore it in our projections.

> Canadians refer to it as the **OAS clawback**. The government calls it the "Old Age Security pension recovery tax." It

involves the federal government taxing back a portion of your OAS pensions when individual net income is over a certain threshold. In 2020, the threshold is $79,054 per individual. You would have to pay back an amount equal to 15 percent of your net 2020 income over this threshold, with the maximum payback being 100 percent of the OAS pension you received. If your net income exceeds $128,137, you have to pay it all back, in which case Old Age Security does nothing for you.

Takeaways

1. Enhancement 1 is hugely important for high-net-worth couples. So is Enhancement 4.
2. Enhancements 2 and 3 also have a positive effect for high-net-worth couples, but they are not nearly as important as they are for middle-income retirees.
3. High-net-worth couples should also defer OAS to 70.

CHAPTER 23

Tax-Sheltered vs. After-Tax Assets

Until Chapter 21, all money saved for retirement was held in tax-assisted vehicles such as RRSPs, RRIFs, and LIFs. With one exception, any amounts saved were tax-deductible and the withdrawals after retirement were subject to income tax.

TFSAs were the exception, as contributions to a TFSA are not tax-deductible and the investment income is not subject to income tax, ever. When money is withdrawn from a TFSA, it is not deemed to be income at all and is therefore not subject to income tax or even the OAS clawback.

In Chapter 21, the Wongs had a source of retirement income — stocks and bonds — that fell outside of any tax-sheltered arrangement. The same was true of the Clarkes in Chapter 22.

Having assets is always a good thing, whether they are tax-sheltered or not, but non-tax-sheltered (NTS) assets add an extra dimension to the decumulation challenge. You must take into account the different tax treatment of each holding and decide when it is best to turn that asset into income.

Dividends and interest earned on NTS assets are taxable at different rates. Both are taxed annually while capital gains are taxable only when the investment is sold. If they had no capital gains on their investments, the Wongs could sell them and spend the proceeds without any tax consequences.

The table below summarizes how tax treatment varies depending on the savings vehicle that the withdrawals came from.

Table 23.1. Tax treatment on withdrawals

Source of the withdrawal	Income tax treatment
RRSP, RRIF, LIF, or annuity purchased with monies from an RRSP	Taxed as ordinary income except a small amount is offset by the pension amount tax credit after age 65
TFSA	Not subject to income tax, ever
NTS assets in brokerage accounts, bank accounts, etc.	Income tax is incurred on the profit if an investment is sold, not by withdrawal

This brings up the burning question of what assets to cash out first in retirement. The goal with a decumulation strategy is to maximize one's *after-tax* income rather than just maximizing income. Doing the latter doesn't necessarily ensure the former.

Monies from after-tax assets (including a TFSA) generally go farther in retirement than monies from tax-sheltered vehicles. For instance, if your marginal tax rate in retirement is 33 percent, then one dollar of income from a TFSA is equivalent to $1.50 of income from a RRIF or a LIF.

All things being equal, you should withdraw your NTS assets first, except for your TFSA, where the investment income accumulates tax-free. Interest income and realized capital gains and losses on other NTS assets are taxable annually whereas the investment income within your RRIF, LIF, or RRSPs is not taxed until the money is withdrawn. Keeping your tax-sheltered monies intact for as long as possible is usually the best way to maximize the growth of your total assets, or at least to minimize net shrinkage.

There are exceptions to this simple rule. For one thing, you might have to sell some stocks or bonds in order to draw income from your NTS assets. If those investments include a large capital gain, selling them can trigger a big tax bill a lot sooner than you would like.

Another constraint is that you want to make maximum use of your tax credits because they do not carry forward. The tax credits I am referring to include the basic personal amount, the age amount, and the pension income amount. To take advantage of these credits, you need to ensure a certain amount of income is derived from tax-sheltered vehicles (not including your TFSA).

By the way, if you purchased an annuity with tax-sheltered assets when you retired (which was Enhancement 3), the annuity income is essentially the same, tax-wise, as withdrawing the money straight from a RRIF.

The OAS clawback presents another interesting wrinkle, assuming you have enough taxable income for it to be an issue. (See p. 147 for details.) If some of your OAS pension is getting clawed back because of your income level, you might consider deferring the start of OAS until 70 and drawing more of your income from other sources before then.

To sum up, you want to structure your withdrawals so that you (a) maximize the use of your tax credits, (b) minimize income tax payable on investment income from NTS assets, and (c) minimize income tax payable as a result of receiving income from your RRIF, LIF, or annuity.

If all that isn't complicated enough, you also want to avoid a significant dip in your after-tax income at some point down the road. For example, say you draw all your income from NTS assets and your TFSA in your early retirement years. That might leave you only with your tax-sheltered assets to produce income in your later years. While that might produce the same amount of gross income, it would be taxed more heavily, resulting in a substantial decline in after-tax income.

For the purposes of the calculations in this book and PERC, I have assumed that income each year in retirement would come from a blend of all the various asset classes. This isn't necessarily the most tax-efficient strategy, so if you have significant NTS and tax-sheltered assets, I suggest you have a discussion with your accountant about how best to draw them down.

Takeaway

1. Ultimately, the real goal is to maximize your after-tax income, not your gross income.

CHAPTER 24

Retiring Single

So far, the focus has been on married couples, but not everyone retires with a spouse. At the risk of oversimplifying, the situation for singles is generally the same except that they will need less money to maintain the same standard of living. And by less money, I don't mean just half as much. Retirement experts tend to agree that a single person generally requires about 70 percent as much income as a married couple to achieve the same standard of living.

Another difference for single people is the annuity. It will cost less than for a couple because it doesn't have to include the cost of lifetime income for the surviving spouse.

To explore other ways in which retirement for singles might be subtly different than for couples, we will use Karen as an example. Karen is 65 with $360,000 in RRSP assets and $60,000 in her TFSA. We will assume that Karen has three spending shocks in total, each a little smaller than what the Thompsons incurred.

Let's first consider the situation where Karen rejects all the enhancements and tries to draw income of $40,000 a year including CPP and OAS. In future years, she increases that draw based on the curve that we established in Chapter 5. As before, we assume she achieves just 5th-percentile investment returns.

Unfortunately, we find that Karen would use up her entire savings by age 80 under this scenario. This is shown in Figure 24.1.

Figure 24.1. Karen's projected income without the enhancements

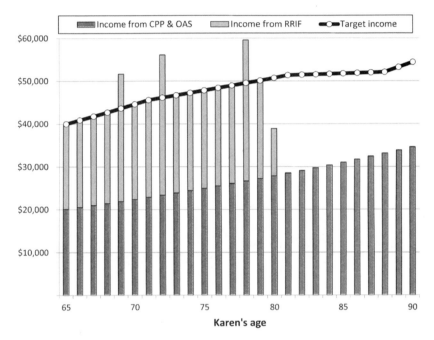

Karen tries to draw total income of $40,000 (plus inflation) with $420,000 in tax-sheltered assets but she didn't adopt the enhancements. This chart includes three spending shocks: $8,000 at age 69, $10,000 at 72, and $10,000 at 78.

If Karen adopts the first three enhancements, the same $420,000 in assets is enough to meet her income needs well into her 80s. The first three enhancements are just as important for single retirees as they are for couples.

In a real-life situation, it is important that Karen also adopt Enhancement 4 (where she uses PERC to monitor and adjust her income on a regular basis). If her investment returns are better than the worst-case scenario, she could draw more income. If she is lucky enough to get investment returns equal to the median return (about 5 percent before fees), she can draw about $46,000 a year.

Figure 24.2. After the three enhancements: worst-case scenario

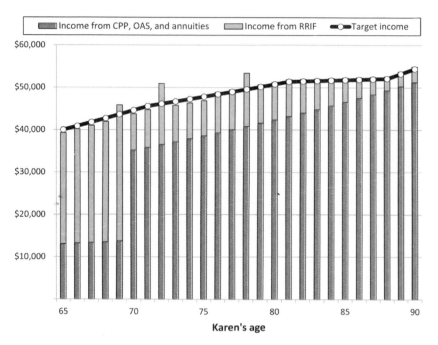

This is the same as Figure 24.1 but assumes that Karen has adopted the first three enhancements. She also set up a reserve to soften the impact of spending shocks.

What this shows is that most of the uncertainty about retirement vanishes for single retirees like Karen if they adopt the enhancements. Her range of expected income is $40,000 to $46,000 with only a tiny chance of it being below this range and a reasonable chance of it exceeding the top end.

The importance of pensions from government sources might make some people a little nervous, but I don't think we need to worry. The odds of the government cutting OAS or CPP are very low. I see this as a good news story in that Karen gets most of her income after age 70 from very secure sources. That income will continue for life, no matter how long she lives.

This example gives further insight into the threshold amount of assets needed to be able to defer CPP to age 70. As was mentioned in Chapter 12, a retiree needs a significant amount of money to be able to wait until 70 to start collecting CPP. In the case of a single retiree who is age 65, the amount is about $300,000 in investable assets. Below that level, the retiree doesn't have enough assets to produce the desired income target curve. If the individual retired at 60, the threshold is a little over $400,000.

Takeaways

1. The enhancements are just as important for single retirees as they are for couples.
2. Government pensions will be a dominant factor for a retiree who is single with less than half a million in assets, especially if she defers CPP until 70. This is a good thing since it takes much of the uncertainty out of decumulation.

CHAPTER 25

Where Do Bequests Fit In?

So far, we have focused on the income needs of the retirees themselves, which is what you would have expected. But what about the potential heirs? Should an intended bequest alter the basic decumulation strategy in some way?

Your first thought might be "Of course it is important to take care of my loved ones. I want to be sure my spouse will be financially secure if I die first." If your spouse's welfare is your concern, then don't worry. The enhancements described in this book are geared toward satisfying the income needs of both spouses, no matter how long they live or who dies first.

This chapter deals with bequests where someone else is the beneficiary, be it your children, grandchildren, or a long-lost nephew.

Accidental Bequests

If you are a single retiree or a surviving spouse, you will usually know precisely who will inherit your money. Typically, the designated beneficiaries receive whatever money remains in the estate on death. In the economic literature, this type of bequest is known as an **accidental bequest**. This is how mainstream retirees and YOLOs usually pass on their remaining wealth when they die.

If this is what you plan to do, then carry on as you were. Unless you promised someone a specific amount, your bequest plans should not affect your decumulation strategy one iota.

Other Bequests

Besides accidental bequests, two other types are described in the literature: altruistic and strategic. The altruistic bequest involves earmarking a certain amount of money to be left to a loved one — usually one's children — out of love and concern for their welfare. It differs from an accidental bequest in that you will tend to have a certain number in mind. This is the type of bequest I would most closely associate with the Cleavers, whom I described in Chapter 18. They will want to be sure that a certain child (now an adult) will be financially secure for as long as they live.

The third type, the strategic bequest, is more like a payoff. You leave money to a person who provided you with attention or care in your latter years, usually when your health starts to fail. That person may or may not be a relative. Once again, you will have a certain number in mind as to the amount of the bequest.

To Make a Bequest or Not

You shouldn't feel guilty if you have not planned an altruistic bequest or if you think the accidental bequest that your heirs can expect will be a smallish number. Not everyone feels the need to enrich their adult children, not even the wealthy.

US Trust conducted a survey in 2012 of 642 high-net-worth adults. All had at least US$3 million in investable assets. The survey results were compiled separately for different age groups, but we will focus solely on the baby boomers. Only 55 percent of them felt it was important to leave money to their children.

Among the 45 percent of baby boomers who did not plan to make a bequest, some of the reasons given were:

- "each generation should earn its own wealth" (57 percent),
- "I worked hard for my wealth and will want to enjoy it myself" (27 percent),
- "I would rather give the money to charity" (26 percent), and
- "it is important to invest in my children's success while they are growing up" (and by implication not after they are grown up).

I can see how the wealthy — like the people who responded to the above survey — would be more likely to make a bequest than couples with more modest means. First, they might feel it is just plain wrong, in some ill-defined way, to be spending so much money on themselves and feel it is only right to pass some of it along to their children. Second, their children might have become accustomed to receiving money throughout their lives and thus have some expectation of receiving more upon the death of the parent.

This brings me to the point I am trying to make. If 45 percent of the wealthy do not feel they have to make a bequest, then surely a much higher percentage of retirees who have much less money (like the Thompsons) should not feel any obligation to do so.

The rest of this chapter is for readers who still intend to make either an altruistic or a strategic bequest of a fixed amount.

Bequests and Home Equity

In most cases, there will be enough equity in your principal residence to handle most strategic bequests as well as many altruistic bequests. Few Canadians think of their home as a financial asset except to the minor extent that they might take out a home equity loan for renovations or a special trip. That changes upon death or, more specifically, upon the death of the last surviving spouse. At that point, the equity in the home is essentially pure cash.

I suggest that you estimate how much your home would be worth if you sold it today, net of commissions and any expenses attached to settling your estate. To be conservative, assume that the value will rise by just 1 or 2 percent a year. If this amount is not enough to handle the bequest you have in mind, then you will either have to reduce the amount of the bequest or divert some of the financial assets that you had earmarked to generate income to meet your own needs.

The safest way to make sure you leave behind enough to cover your strategic or altruistic bequest is to hold back some assets when entering information into PERC to figure out how much income you can draw. The amount you hold back, when added to the equity in your home, is the minimum amount that would be available upon death.

How Bequests Might Change with Age

Most bequests will vary over time. You are not the only one who is getting older; so are your designated beneficiaries. For example, say you have a child who is now age 40 and needs financial assistance for the rest of his life. The amount of money needed to cover his costs for the rest of his life would be very large indeed. Your existing assets would have to be substantial if you are currently financing his needs. If you died in 20 years' time, your assets will probably have shrunk somewhat, but that child would now be 60 and the amount of money needed to meet his needs would also have shrunk. The calculations are beyond the scope of this book and are not contemplated by PERC. The point here is that your ability to finance your child's special needs might be diminishing over time but so is the quantum of those needs. I cannot promise, however, that they are shrinking at the same rate.

What About Inheritances?

Until now, the discussion has been about how you might give away your money after death and to whom. What about if you are on the receiving end? Perhaps an elderly parent is still alive and you have reason to think you are going to be a beneficiary in the will. Should you take that potential inheritance into account before you have the money in your hands?

There is an obvious danger in building your financial plans around an inheritance that might happen later than you think or that might not happen at all. Mom might need some expensive long-term care in her final years, which could consume her entire wealth. Or in a fit of pique, she might end up giving the entire inheritance to your younger sister.

The safest thing to do is to ignore a potential inheritance when entering your asset information into PERC. On the other hand, we have already built a good deal of pessimism into our model by assuming 5th-percentile investment returns. It may not be such a bad idea to factor in a positive financial event if it is almost certain to occur. PERC allows for it. Just be cautious about estimating the amount you expect to get or how soon you might receive it.

Takeaways

1. Most bequests are accidental in nature, meaning that the names of the heirs are known but the amount being inherited is not guaranteed.

2. In the case of retirees who have substantial equity in their home and otherwise follow the decumulation strategy in this book, their heirs can expect to receive a significant if unspecified amount on the death of the surviving spouse.

3. You pay a price for making a large bequest. It can restrict your choice of investment vehicles at retirement and reduce your retirement income.

4. You should be drawing down your financial assets as you get older, which means any accidental bequest will gradually become smaller. Your children's need for the money should also diminish as they progress into later adulthood.

5. Be cautious about taking into account a potential future inheritance when calculating your retirement income. Note, though, that PERC allows for it.

PART IV

Making It Happen

You now know what can go wrong in retirement and how to avoid the trouble. But how do you make the ideal decumulation strategy a reality without becoming a retirement expert? And if you are an employer who sponsors a defined contribution retirement plan, what is the best way to help your employees turn their account balances into a predictable stream of retirement income?

CHAPTER 26

Lingering Doubts?

In this book, I have set out a decumulation strategy that will keep you solvent even if you experience poor investment returns or live longer than you expected. And even if neither of these things happen, you will still do well with the enhancements I have described.

Yet, you might still have that small voice in the back of your head telling you this doesn't feel quite right. After all, if these strategies are supposed to be so effective, why haven't you heard about them before now? I hope this chapter puts your mind to rest.

The Framing Effect

If you put yourself in the shoes of Nick and Susan, you know you should be feeling much better about your retirement prospects after seeing the effect of the enhancements, but maybe that isn't the case. Some of the enhancements admittedly go against the grain — especially CPP deferral and purchasing an annuity. As a result, you might be inclined to look for a reason to reject them. This could be true even if you cannot refute the arguments I have made in their favour. It is sort of like witnessing a magic trick that you cannot explain but still leaves you incredulous.

If this is where you're coming from, the framing effect may have something to do with it. We all have preconceived notions of right and wrong. These notions are often useful in our lives, but sometimes they get in the way of our acting in our best interests. When it comes to decumulation, we should always make decisions that produce the best outcome, but this is often not what happens. The way a question or a problem is framed can dramatically affect how we respond to it.

Consider a classic experiment by psychologists Daniel Kahneman and Amos Tversky, two giants in the field of behavioural science. In the experiment, test subjects were told that 600 people have a disease for which there are two possible treatments: Treatment A and Treatment B. The subjects were divided into two groups and each group was given a different explanation of the treatments.

The subjects in Group 1 were told that Treatment A would save 200 lives. As for Treatment B, there was a 33-1/3-percent chance that everyone would be saved and a 66-2/3-percent chance that no one would be saved. Based on this explanation, 72 percent of the subjects in Group 1 chose Treatment A.

In the case of the subjects in Group 2, it was explained that 400 patients would die under Treatment A, while Treatment B offered a 33-1/3-percent chance that no one would die and a 66-2/3-percent chance that everyone would die. Given these facts, only 22 percent chose Treatment A!

Take a minute to wrap your mind around the question. The explanations are presenting precisely the same facts; they differ only in the choice of words. In theory, Group 1 and Group 2 subjects should respond the same way whether they heard the first explanation or the second, but that isn't what happened. How a question is asked can fundamentally change our decision, even though the basic underlying facts are the same.

The framing effect has some major implications for retirement planning. Consider, for example, the natural aversion almost everyone has to annuities. Annuities don't offer any flexibility if an emergency comes up and you need extra cash. In addition, they are a terrible choice if you die soon after buying one.*

---

*   Assuming you didn't provide for a survivor benefit.

Neither of these facts is in dispute. But consider members of public unions and their feelings about their defined benefit (DB) plans. Virtually every union member swears by his DB plan and wouldn't give it up for the world. Non-union employees wish they had a DB plan and pension experts bemoan the fact that employers are shutting down the DB plans they used to offer. Everyone loves DB plans because they provide a completely predictable amount of income and they will pay that income for life.

The thing is, a DB plan is essentially the same thing as an annuity. The only difference is the words used to describe the two vehicles. This is another example of the framing effect at work.

Over time, we develop strong feelings about certain concepts, institutions, or products. Some we perceive as intrinsically good and others as equally bad. If your financial advisor asked you point-blank if you want to buy an annuity or defer your CPP pension, your answer would almost certainly be no. Alternatively, if she asks if you want to be sure you never run out of money during your lifetime, your answer would be yes. Her solution, though, might involve buying an annuity or deferring your CPP pension. By this point, the readers of this book should be able to get past the framing effect and be prepared to make use of all the available tools to achieve their financial goals.

Corroboration

If the decumulation ideas presented in this book are so effective, you might be wondering why you don't hear much about them in the articles you read or from the financial advisors you know. That could be because there is a great divide between the academics and the practitioners in the field. The academics accept these ideas, but they tend not to communicate directly with the general public.

The Stanford Center on Longevity, in collaboration with the Society of Actuaries, prepared a guide for plan sponsors to help them implement defined contribution (DC) retirement programs.[1] While this was an American paper, the basic principles apply equally in Canada. The guide points out the value of deferring government-provided pensions and the role of annuities, two of the basic enhancements that we have analyzed at length in this book.

The Canadian Institute of Actuaries and its representatives have long recognized the importance of keeping fees low when saving for retirement (Enhancement 1). The Association of Canadian Pension Management (ACPM) has taken a leadership role in decumulation. In one paper, the ACPM addresses the issues of high investment fees in retail products, the purchase of annuities, and the merits of delaying CPP benefits.[2] Beyond that, a number of other Canadian academic papers deal with these issues and come to very similar conclusions.

The trouble is that these professional bodies and academics don't seem to be connecting with retirees and so the message has not filtered down to the general public. This book is an attempt to change that.

Takeaway

1. The decumulation strategies presented in this book are widely accepted in the academic community.

CHAPTER 27

Making the Strategy a Reality

Congratulations on making it this far! I assume you are now ready to put the enhancements into practice, which brings us to the practical question of how best to do that. Let's consider the matter one enhancement at a time.

Enhancement 1: Reducing Fees

As I explained in Chapter 10, it is important to keep your investment management fees low. When I speak of investment fees, I include not only the fee to participate in a pooled fund or ETF but also the ongoing fee that would be charged by your financial advisor, if you have one.

You should try to get your overall investment fee down to about 0.6 percent a year, if not less. I see two ways to do this.

The easier path is to use the services of a robo-advisor (also known as an "automated investment advisor"). A robo-advisor is a firm that establishes and maintains your investment portfolio with minimal human supervision, all based on information that you provide online. One such firm is Wealthsimple. The Big-5 banks are also getting involved, such as RBC with its InvestEase platform.

You pay the robo-advisor between 0.2 percent and 0.5 percent a year as a management fee, depending on the firm and the amount of money you are giving them to manage. You pay another 0.2 percent or so to access the advisor's exchange-traded funds (ETFs), though some of the funds in its stable will be more expensive. This brings the total fee to something close to the 0.6 percent that we want based on Enhancement 1.

The robo-advisor route is a pretty simple one to follow. Choose a company based on a recommendation from someone you trust or maybe interview two or three of them. If you pick a standalone firm like Wealthsimple, you will want to know how many similar clients they have, their process for getting you started, and what sort of recourse you have to a licensed professional if you run into a problem. These are also questions to ask if you choose the robo-advisor arm of a Big-5 bank, though you at least have the assurance that they have substantial resources behind them.

Once you have selected a firm, the next step involves filling in and submitting an application online. If you're having trouble with the questions, you can usually call for assistance. Licensed portfolio managers should be available to help you, but I don't know of any robo-advisors who would assign a dedicated client representative to be there for you on an ongoing basis. Remember that human intervention is expensive, which is why the robo-advisors try to minimize it.

The submission you make establishes your risk tolerance and goals and then an algorithm turns it into a portfolio of low-cost funds. You do not have to choose funds yourself (in fact, you usually can't). You need not worry about how your asset mix might drift over time since the robo-advisor will monitor it and adjust the mix to stay within the guidelines established when you first submitted your application. On an annual basis, the robo-advisor should be contacting you to update your data and goals. Since one tends to become more risk-averse with age, these annual updates to your profile can result in changes to your portfolio over time. If you want to see how your investments are doing, this is also something you can do online.

The robo-advisor route involves little human contact, and that little you do get will largely be over the phone. This can be distressing to investors who are used to having a real human they can deal with on a regular basis. In addition, you are responsible for making sure nothing falls between the cracks. For instance, it is largely up to you to ensure you comply with the RRSP contribution limits. All that said, if you are reasonably comfortable with e-commerce and remain vigilant, you should have no trouble investing with a robo-advisor.

Enhancement 2: Deferring CPP to 70

Unlike the first enhancement, Enhancement 2 is rather easy to put into practice: you simply wait until you are closing in on age 70 to apply for your CPP benefit. The bigger question is whether this enhancement is right for you. It would be nice if you could talk to a financial advisor who accepts the ideas in this book and who knows your situation intimately, but that may be hard to arrange. Your best bet is to read Chapters 11 and 12 carefully to confirm you are a suitable candidate for Enhancement 2. If your assets are a little less than the amount needed for full CPP deferral, you might be better off deferring CPP to some age between 65 and 70, not 70 itself.

Enhancement 3: Buying an Annuity

In Chapter 13, I showed how the purchase of an annuity could potentially help a couple like the Thompsons. It acts like an insurance policy against two significant risks: having poor investment returns and living longer than you expected. I cannot blame you if you are reluctant to proceed with this enhancement. As I indicated in Chapter 13, annuities do not look as attractive as they used to. The main argument in their favour used to be that if you are prepared to invest in long-term bonds, then you should also be willing to buy an annuity. Unfortunately, I no longer regard long-term bonds as such a great investment. I might change my mind on this issue someday, if real interest rates rise again.

If you do decide to go ahead and buy an annuity, you will have to go through a broker or financial advisor to do so. They will charge a commission for their trouble, and there is no reason you cannot ask what that commission is. It might be negotiable. If you have a spouse, be sure to buy an annuity that continues (at about the two-thirds level) to the surviving spouse no matter who dies first.

Enhancement 4: Knowing How Much Income to Draw

Enhancement 4 consists of using a retirement income calculator like PERC on a regular basis, perhaps once a year. As I have mentioned elsewhere, this is the most important of all the enhancements. With the help of Morneau Shepell,* I hope to continue to maintain PERC in the long run, and even to improve on it. There are many other retirement income calculators out there but, to my knowledge, PERC is the only one that explicitly takes the first three enhancements into account. Also, it doesn't require you to enter your email address or to provide confidential information. If you are like me, you don't need to be placed on more marketing mailing lists!

Enhancement 5: Have a Backstop

If you accept the first four enhancements, you will probably never have to worry about implementing Enhancement 5, getting extra income by taking out a reverse mortgage. It is there to help you only in the most extreme circumstances. As I indicated earlier, I see the purpose of a reverse mortgage as a means to *maintain* your lifestyle, not to raise it to a higher level. On the other hand, who am I to judge? If you are 80, have a lot of equity locked up in your principal residence, and have no need to leave money to others, then why not spend more in your remaining years?

---

* Morneau Shepell's IT people helped me to make PERC available to the public online at perc.morneaushepell.com.

Financial Advisors

In the last chapter, I indicated that many industry experts and professional associations already endorse the enhancements that are presented in this book. Unfortunately, most financial advisors are a conspicuous exception.

There are a couple of possible reasons for their general reluctance to embrace the enhancements outlined in Part II. One is that they learned traditional strategies years ago that are less applicable today. For instance, deferring CPP until 70 is far more important today, with lower interest rates and longer life expectancies, than would have been the case 20 years ago.

The second reason has to do with how financial advisors are compensated. Most of them receive a percentage of assets as their fee and so their interests are not aligned with yours during the decumulation stage. It is easy to see why they wouldn't be thrilled with Enhancement 1 (reduced fees) or Enhancement 2 (deferring CPP, which draws down your savings more quickly). They won't even like Enhancement 3 much; an annuity purchase provides a commission, but it is a one-time event that reduces the advisor's ongoing revenue stream. The same goes with Enhancement 5, reverse mortgages.

The only enhancement that doesn't reduce their compensation is Enhancement 4 (dynamic spending), but this is not financially rewarding to financial advisors. They do not get paid extra to help you adjust your spending, and using this tool can involve a lot of extra time and effort on their part.

On the other hand, I know a growing number of financial advisors out there who do accept these ideas, and you may be lucky enough to find one. Also, you may need a financial advisor for many other reasons, such as setting up a trust, finding the most tax-effective solution, establishing your will, or reviewing your insurance needs in retirement. Consequently, you may want to give a financial advisor a try. You might even suggest they read a copy of this book if they haven't seen it yet.

I am less optimistic about this approach if your advisor has put you into mutual funds that contain a deferred sales charge (DSC). To me, this is one of the most odious practices a fund salesperson can perpetrate on an innocent investor. DSCs saddle you with high fees and take away the freedom to move your monies from one fund family to another. Do not trust anyone who has recommended investment funds with a DSC.

> A **deferred sales charge (DSC)** is a rather large commission that a mutual fund salesperson receives upfront. If you change your mind and try to move to another fund family within a certain period (about six years), you are charged a hefty redemption penalty. On $500,000 of investments, the fee could be $20,000 or more. The salesperson may say it is for your own protection — so you don't jump from one investment to another too often — but this is like an employer saying that he locks in his employees at night "for their own protection."

The Employer Route

It is possible that you accumulated most of your savings in an employer-sponsored group plan. This would be either a group RRSP or a defined contribution pension plan. If your employer provides ongoing support after retirement at no cost to you, you should probably take them up on it. In my experience, employers tend to have your best interests at heart; they can also provide you with access to objective expertise at reasonable cost.

The support may include ongoing investment education and help with your decumulation strategy. You should also see if you can keep your money in the employer-sponsored retirement plan after retirement. But do ask about the investment management fees before you sign on.

Takeaways

1. There are four ways to bring to life the decumulation strategy recommended in this book: using a robo-advisor, the DIY approach, through traditional financial advisors, or through your employer.

2. The DIY approach is cheapest, but you need to navigate around the pitfalls. It is not for the novice or the faint of heart.

3. Financial advisors are the most natural source for help, but the solutions presented in this book may conflict with how they are remunerated. In addition, the cost of an advisor offsets the benefits of Enhancement 1.

4. If you accumulated most of your savings through a workplace plan, your employer may be prepared to offer ongoing support, at least to see you through the transition into retirement. You should probably use it.

5. Robo-advisors may be the most sensible route for most retirees.

CHAPTER 28

A Message for Employers

If you are an employer who sponsors a defined contribution (DC) pension plan for your employees, or maybe a group RRSP, give yourself a pat on the back. You are ensuring that your employees are among the "haves" in a land that is too heavily populated with "have-nots" when it comes to pension coverage. Barely 20 percent of employees in the private sector are covered by a pension plan, be it defined benefit (DB) or defined contribution.*

Never mind the barrage of criticism from labour groups and academics that DC plans are inadequate because they subject employees to too much risk. This is the 21st century and individuals need to shoulder some responsibility for their own welfare. What you are offering your employees with your DC plan is much needed help to achieve retirement income security. Moreover, as I showed in Part II, a DC plan can come close to providing as much predictability of income as a DB plan if one uses a good decumulation strategy.

---

* A mandatory group RRSP with employer contributions is almost as good. That would raise the coverage rate to nearly 30 percent.

To be clear, I do not criticize employers for having pulled out of DB pension plans over the past 30 years; DB proved to be unsustainable in the private sector. The problem I have with DC plans is that too many sponsors think their role ends when an employee retires.

The Next Step

In your role as plan sponsor, you provided significant support during the accumulation phase. You made regular contributions to the pension plan, offered a variety of investment options at an attractive low cost, and provided ongoing education to plan participants. With the emerging role of auto-enrolment and improved default options, employees don't even need to understand investment basics or retirement planning to accumulate an impressive account balance by retirement.

This is commendable, but why stop there? At the present time, employer support is usually restricted to the accumulation phase. When an employee retires, he finds himself on his own when it comes to finding someone to manage his monies. As the former employer and sponsor of the DC plan the money came from, you could help the new retiree to assess the suitability of the options being made available by the next service provider, or the fees being charged. But for the most part, you don't. The retiring employee is given no communication or decision tools to guide him. Instead, he is given a deadline by which time his monies must be moved out.

The accumulation phase is certainly important, but as I have emphasized time and again in this book, the decumulation phase is just as crucial and a lot more challenging. Consider the words of William Sharpe, professor of finance, emeritus, at Stanford University, who is one of the originators of the capital asset pricing model, the creator of the Sharpe ratio for the analysis of risk-adjusted investment performance, and the 1990 winner of the Nobel Prize in Economics. In a speech at the 2014 CFA Institute annual conference, Professor Sharpe said retirement income planning "is a really hard problem. It's the hardest problem I've ever looked at." If Nobel Prize winners have trouble with retirement planning, how can you leave your employees to pursue it unaided?

It is the rare individual who can navigate the dangerous waters of decumulation alone. And in far too many cases, that individual may not be much better off in the hands of a financial advisor or mutual fund salesperson whose interests are not aligned with those of the retiree.

The Business Case for Pension Plans

As an employer, it can be useful to remember why your company established a pension plan in the first place. If it was long ago, it may have been to attract and retain employees, but these reasons no longer hold water. In a defined contribution world, a pension plan is not much of a retention tool since departing employees can bring their account balances with them. And the ability of a pension plan to attract talent is overrated; far more important to prospective employees are salary, non-pension benefits, and prospects for advancement.

So why do you still sponsor a pension plan? I suspect the main reason is inertia, or perhaps we can call it the path of least resistance; it is easier to keep a plan going that was started decades ago than to terminate it and deal with employees' inevitable disgruntlement.

You have a better reason to continue sponsoring a pension plan than inertia, even if it is a DC plan: you want to see your employees do well after retirement. This is not altruistic sentiment. It is good business.

Imagine an employee who has worked diligently for your organization for 20 or 30 years. If there was no pension plan and she did not save enough on her own, she would be facing a significant drop in her standard of living. Most likely, she would be forced to sell her home and move to a smaller place in a less attractive area. She might even resort to relying on handouts from church groups or family members to make ends meet.

If this was the typical fate of employees in your organization, your company's public image would take a beating. Equally important, you couldn't expect to get the best performance out of your employees who are still active. They might not have given the company pension plan much thought when they were first hired, but they are unlikely to give you their best work effort later in their careers if they feel you do not care about them. So ultimately, sponsoring a pension plan is about enhancing the corporate image, boosting morale, and improving productivity. As reasons go, these are very good ones.

Reasons Given for Not Helping Retirees

Given the above business case for maintaining a pension plan, it is easy to see that your role should not end at the point of retirement. If you really want your employees to retire well and ensure they do not outlive their money, you should continue to guide them in the decumulation phase. Yet the norm is still to focus only on the accumulation phase and to leave employees to their own devices at the point of retirement.

Employers are leery about taking on fiduciary liability for the period after retirement, since it might expose them to litigation. In my opinion, though, the exposure is minor relative to the reward. It is also minor relative to the financial risk to some DB plan sponsors in terms of the volatility of their pension expense. In any event, safeguards can be put in place to limit the employer's exposure even further in this regard, as will be shown below in the solution section.

Another reason not to act has to do with legislative restrictions, but this has become more of a historical problem. Until recently, some provinces did not allow employers to offer in-plan decumulation solutions. The remaining legal barriers toward in-plan decumulation have been taken down, and it is only a matter of time before plan sponsors start to do more to support their retirees. No other scenario can be justified. If this book has shown anything, it is that individual employees are not going to stumble onto a smart decumulation strategy on their own.

A third reason that most employers have not yet acted is they are getting little pressure from their employees to help more. Is this surprising? There is little awareness that alternatives exist, and in such a vacuum it is human nature to accept with some forbearance the circumstances in which we find ourselves. I remember when I was 13 that it took me longer to copy work from the blackboard than my classmates. I also missed more fly balls when I was out in the schoolyard. I had become quite myopic but, until I put on a pair of glasses, I didn't realize it. Until retiring employees put on their decumulation glasses and see the fresh possibilities, they are in the same position.

The fourth and final reason that employers have been slow to act is that the solutions have been slow to present themselves. This is changing. Effective solutions are now being created, and the good news is that they do not have to result in additional costs to the employer. Employers are using their buying power to give their employees access to institutional-level fees, which is quite a godsend. The fees that retiring employees incur for actively managed investment funds can be slashed to less than a third of what they would be charged in the retail market for traditional mutual funds.

What Should a Good Solution Look Like?

Employers are in a unique position to assist their retiring employees. They have the benefit of economy of scale to provide investment options at institutional rates that are a fraction of retail fees. They can do the same with making annuities available. And they can employ outside expertise at reasonable cost to offer unbiased, cutting-edge decumulation solutions, such as the ones presented in this book.

Some Canadian organizations have already shown leadership in this area and have implemented decumulation options within their retirement programs. Those options range from payment of variable pensions out of the plan to the establishment of group LIFs and group RRIFs. This is only the beginning.

Companies like Morneau Shepell are on the threshold of a next-generation response to the decumulation challenges faced by retirees. The solutions being proposed include some or all of the following elements:

- An array of passively managed, low-cost investment funds that allow the retiree to construct a diversified portfolio with his retirement savings.
- Assistance in establishing the asset mix for such a fund.
- Assistance in determining the appropriate percentage of assets to allocate for the purchase of an annuity and seeking the best price available in the insurance marketplace.
- A call centre to answer ongoing questions.

- An annual checkup that includes a review of the financial position of the retiree and whether the income withdrawal rate should be adjusted.
- Lower fees thanks to economies of scale.

Takeaways

1. Employers have an excellent business case for maintaining a pension plan for their employees. It indirectly results in better employee performance as well as a better public image for the organization.
2. That same business case strongly suggests that employer support should continue beyond retirement.
3. There are a variety of reasons why employers currently help so little during the decumulation phase, but the tide is turning.

APPENDIX A

Summary of Takeaways

The most important takeaways are highlighted in **boldface**.

Chapter	Takeaway
1	**This book is for people who are close to retirement, or who are already retired, and who are going to rely heavily on their own savings to meet their retirement income needs.**
	It is assumed that your primary goal is to maximize your retirement income rather than maximizing the assets you leave behind if you die early.
2	A conventional decumulation strategy sounds like a prudent course to follow, but it can lead to disaster.
3	Decumulation is not as straightforward as it seems; disaster can strike even if you save a lot and follow a widely accepted decumulation strategy.
	The 4-percent rule doesn't work when investment returns are very poor.

4   Most spending shocks that you are likely to encounter in retirement are modest enough to be manageable.

The biggest spending shocks tend to be events involving family members, like divorce or extending financial support to a grown-up child.

Contribute 3 to 5 percent of your income to a reserve fund until age 75 or so, and use this reserve to cover spending shocks.

5   **Spending by retirees tends to rise more slowly than inflation, especially between ages 70 and 90.** This is true even if they have the financial means to spend more.

6   Investment losses will happen every so often; a good decumulation strategy should be able to absorb them.

Withdrawing the same percentage of assets each year does not work well. In general, you need to withdraw an increasing percentage of your assets with age.

Most retirees want to leave the principal amount of their nest egg intact, but this strategy makes sense only at the extremes of wealth.

Withdrawing the minimum amount permitted under the RRIF rules is not a bad decumulation strategy, but you can do better.

7   **Future investment returns will almost certainly be lower than historical returns for many years to come.**

You might be able to avoid 5th-percentile investment returns by putting all your money in a savings account.

Stay away from investing in second mortgages.

Real estate investing can be lucrative for long-term investors, but it is not for amateurs and it is not without risks.

You might invest some of your savings in T-bills or other short-term investments but only a smallish portion.

Long-term bonds will be especially poor performers, since bond yields have nowhere to go but up, and this would create capital losses. This includes real return bonds.

Your best bet for a 5 percent annual return is to invest in equity funds, risky as they are.

A 60-40 asset mix is probably better than 50-50 in the case of retirees with average risk tolerance.

8   Black swan events can lead to unusually severe bear markets that can disrupt your retirement planning.

The last 70 years of bear markets suggest it is best to stay fully invested during a market downturn, but a bear market brought on by a black swan event may be different.

You might consider reducing your equity exposure on the way down but only if you are prepared to miss the subsequent market recovery.

9   Before embarking on the enhancements, you should get your finances in order by going through the checklist.

10   Reducing investment fees can significantly increase one's retirement income.

Actively managed funds are more expensive than passively managed funds, like ETFs, but with no evidence that they add value when you take fees into account.

Using passively managed ETFs, the total annual investment fee can be brought down to about 0.45 to 0.6 percent if you use a robo-advisor, less if you do it all yourself.

11   Deferring CPP pension to age 70 forces you to draw down your RRIF assets (or other assets) more quickly before age 70, but those same assets last longer because the CPP pension from age 70 and on is so much bigger.

Enhancement 2 greatly reduces the income gap at older ages for middle-income couples like the Thompsons.

12 **Enhancement 2 provides significant protection against investment risk as well as longevity risk.**

There are many reasons for not deferring CPP pension to age 70, but most of them do not hold up to close scrutiny.

About the only good reason not to defer CPP to 70 is having insufficient assets to tide you over until CPP starts.

You probably will not want to defer your OAS pension unless your income after 65 is high enough to be subject to the OAS clawback rules.

13 **If you have a spouse and intend to buy an annuity, it should be a joint and survivor annuity so that payments continue to be made to the surviving spouse.**

Don't even think about buying an indexed annuity.

Buying an annuity is not as effective a strategy as it used to be now that interest rates are so low. That can change, though.

You should be earmarking about 20 percent of your tax-sheltered assets for the purchase of an annuity at the point of retirement.

It is tempting to wait until you're older, like 75, to buy an annuity and in fact you'll be better off than buying one at 65 *assuming* you don't suffer any investment losses in the interim. This, however, is a dangerous assumption to make.

While it is early days, an ALDA does not look like a very effective retirement income vehicle.

14 **Enhancement 1 is a no-brainer.**

We already know that Enhancements 2 and 3 should help in a worst-case scenario because both are a form of insurance against poor returns and a long lifespan.

What is a bonus is finding that Enhancements 2 and 3 add value even if one achieves median investment returns.

15 **Without knowing how much income you can safely draw each year, Enhancements 2 and 3 are virtually useless.**

You can use PERC (an online calculator) to determine how much income you can draw from all sources.

There is no charge to use PERC.

It is important to revisit PERC on a regular basis, say annually.

16 If all else fails, a reverse mortgage can provide much-needed income late in retirement.

It is better not to secure a reverse mortgage too early. Wait until age 75 or so but don't wait too long.

For a retiree, a reverse mortgage is generally a more viable option than a HELOC.

17 Enhancements 2 and 3 are essentially insurance against living a very long life.

Even if one spouse dies young, the surviving spouse is still financially better off if the couple had adopted Enhancements 2 and 3 at the point of retirement.

18 There are at least two other types of retirees, Super-Savers and YOLOs. The decumulation strategy presented in Part II works for them as well, but with some tweaks.

19 Retiring early is much more of a challenge than waiting until age 65. Not only do your savings produce much less income, you pay more in income tax.

If you retire early, it takes much more assets to put Enhancement 2 into effect.

If you stop working before age 65, you are still better off waiting until 65 or later to collect CPP (assuming you have enough other assets), in spite of the dilution caused by a few more years of no CPP contributions.

20   PERC can be a useful tool to tweak your retirement planning if you still plan to work a few more years.

21   PERC is useful in taking an assortment of "lumpy" assets from many sources and turning them into a smooth income stream.

      If you want to create a smooth income stream, you may have to sell off illiquid assets such as an investment property, sooner than you otherwise would.

22   Enhancement 1 is hugely important for high-net-worth couples. So is Enhancement 4.

      Enhancements 2 and 3 also have a positive effect for high-net-worth couples, but they are not nearly as important as they are for middle-income retirees.

      High-net-worth couples should also defer OAS to 70.

23   Ultimately, the real goal is to maximize your after-tax income, not your gross income.

24   The enhancements are just as important for single retirees as they are for couples.

      Government pensions will be a dominant factor for a retiree who is single with less than half a million in assets, especially if she defers CPP until 70. This is a good thing since it takes much of the uncertainty out of decumulation.

25   Most bequests are accidental in nature, meaning that the names of the heirs are known but the amount being inherited is not guaranteed.

      In the case of retirees who have substantial equity in their home and otherwise follow the decumulation strategy in this book, their heirs can expect to receive a significant if unspecified amount on the death of the surviving spouse.

You pay a price for making a large bequest. It can restrict your choice of investment vehicles at retirement and reduce your retirement income.

You should be drawing down your financial assets as you get older, which means any accidental bequest will gradually become smaller. Your children's need for the money should also diminish as they progress into later adulthood.

Be cautious about taking into account a potential future inheritance when calculating your retirement income. Note, though, that PERC allows for it.

26   The decumulation strategies presented in this book are widely accepted in the academic community.

27   There are four ways to bring to life the decumulation strategy recommended in this book: using a robo-advisor, the DIY approach, through traditional financial advisors, or through your employer.

The DIY approach is cheapest, but you need to navigate around the pitfalls. It is not for the novice or the faint of heart.

Financial advisors are the most natural source for help, but the solutions presented in this book may conflict with how they are remunerated. In addition, the cost of an advisor offsets the benefits of Enhancement 1.

If you accumulated most of your savings through a workplace plan, your employer may be prepared to offer ongoing support, at least to see you through the transition into retirement. You should probably use it.

Robo-advisors may be the most sensible route for most retirees.

28   Employers have an excellent business case for maintaining a pension plan for their employees. It indirectly results in better employee performance as well as a better public image for the organization.

That same business case strongly suggests that employer support should continue beyond retirement.

There are a variety of reasons why employers currently help so little during the decumulation phase, but the tide is turning.

APPENDIX B

Summary of LIFs and RRIFs

This appendix summarizes the rules for the various registered retirement vehicles you might use during the decumulation phase. I am grateful to Tess Francis and Jamie Golombek from CIBC's financial planning division for providing me with the benefit of their research and insights.

Overview

The vehicle you use in the decumulation phase depends in part on where the money came from. If you were saving for retirement in an RRSP, the money will eventually be transferred to a RRIF, used to purchase a life annuity, or some combination of the two. You can also transfer monies initially to a RRIF and then decide a few years later to buy an annuity with some or all of the remaining RRIF assets.

If the savings vehicle was a DC pension plan, the decumulation vehicle will probably be a life income fund (LIF) or equivalent (some provinces call it something else). I say probably because you may have the option of keeping the monies in your employer's pension plan. This might be a very good thing to do because your employer's plan will probably charge lower fees. Alternatively, you can use your DC pension plan balance to buy an annuity. We will ignore the annuity option here because it was addressed in Chapter 13.

RRIF Basics

A RRIF is very much like an RRSP operating in reverse. The basic purpose of an RRSP is to build your retirement savings whereas the purpose of a RRIF is to draw it down; you cannot contribute to a RRIF. What the two vehicles have in common is the choice of investment options and the fact that the investment income is tax-deferred.

When you are ready to start drawing an income, you would close your RRSP account and transfer those assets to a RRIF. This rollover into a RRIF occurs tax-free. You must start making minimum withdrawals from your RRIF by December 31 of the following year. Once you start, the amount you withdraw each year cannot be less than a minimum percentage that varies depending on your age. These percentages are shown in Table B.1 and are applied to the RRIF balance at the end of the previous year.* Withdrawals can be made once a year, semi-annually, quarterly, or monthly.** Additional withdrawals are also permitted. You could also choose to withdraw the entire RRIF balance in one year.

If you do not need the RRIF income, it may be best to keep the money in your RRSP. You no longer have that choice, however, when you turn 71. Your RRSP must be closed by December 31 of the year in which you turn 71 and the amount transferred to a RRIF. You don't have to make a withdrawal from the RRIF until December 31 of the following calendar year. As a result, your first withdrawal from a RRIF does not have to occur until you are 72.

---

* This table ignores the special temporary rules in effect in 2020 in which the usual minimum withdrawal amounts were reduced by 25 percent to reflect the severe bear market conditions that occurred early in the year.

** If you like formulas, the minimum withdrawal between ages 50 and 70 is derived by taking your RRIF balance at the start of the year and dividing it by X, where X = (90 − age). Withdrawals before 55 are not shown here.

Table B.1. Minimum annual withdrawals from an RRIF

Age	Min. annual withdrawal	Age	Min. annual withdrawal
55	2.86%	76	5.98%
56	2.94%	77	6.17%
57	3.03%	78	6.36%
58	3.13%	79	6.58%
59	3.23%	80	6.82%
60	3.33%	81	7.08%
61	3.45%	82	7.38%
62	3.57%	83	7.71%
63	3.70%	84	8.08%
64	3.85%	85	8.51%
65	4.00%	86	8.99%
66	4.17%	87	9.55%
67	4.35%	88	10.21%
68	4.55%	89	10.99%
69	4.76%	90	11.92%
70	5.00%	91	13.06%
71	5.28%	92	14.49%
72	5.40%	93	16.34%
73	5.53%	94	18.79%
74	5.67%	95	20%
75	5.82%	Over 95	20%

It is important to note that you have the option to base your minimum withdrawals on your spouse's age rather than your own age. This can be useful if your spouse is younger and you are trying to minimize your RRIF withdrawals. For example, if you were 72 on January 1, the minimum payout from your RRIF that year would normally be 5.40 percent. If your spouse was age 66, for example, your minimum payout that year could be reduced to 4.17 percent.

RRIF Investments

A RRIF isn't an investment itself. It is an account that holds investments. A RRIF can be invested in a daily interest account, GICs, mutual funds, ETFs, or individual stocks and bonds.

Taxation of a RRIF

All withdrawals from a RRIF are considered taxable income. For tax purposes, however, transfers between vehicles are not considered to be withdrawals. As a result, the one-time rollover from an RRSP to a RRIF is not taxed, nor is the use of RRIF assets to purchase an annuity.

If you draw the minimum amount from a RRIF in a given year, you do not have to pay a withholding tax. If you withdraw more than the minimum amount, the withholding tax on the excess withdrawal is calculated based on the rates in Table B.2. Note that in the first calendar year of the RRIF, the minimum withdrawal is nil, which means tax will be withheld on the entire amount you withdraw.

Table B.2. Withholding tax

Excess withdrawn	Withholding tax*
Up to $5,000	10%
$5,000 to $15,000	20%
Over $15,000	30%

*Different percentages apply in Quebec.

Withdrawals in Kind

If you are withdrawing only the minimum from your RRIF and do not need the money immediately, you can transfer it "in kind" to a TFSA or a non-registered account. This can be useful if all the money in the RRIF is fully invested and you don't want to pay redemption fees or other transaction fees by liquidating it before making the withdrawal. Your institution might still require you to pay a redemption fee, and you are still required to report the in-kind transfer as taxable income.

When You Die

If you have a spouse at the time of death, your spouse can become the owner of your RRIF and would receive future payments, assuming you make the appropriate beneficiary designation. If the amount is rolled over into your spouse's RRSP, RRIF, or annuity, income tax is deferred. Your spouse is subject to income tax on those monies only when withdrawals are made.

If you have no spouse, the RRIF must be collapsed on death and the proceeds paid to your named beneficiary or, if there is none, to your estate. The amount would be fully taxable except if the beneficiary is a financially dependent child or grandchild who is (a) under 18 or (b) dependent due to an infirmity.

Leaving Canada?

If you ever decide to leave Canada permanently, you are generally deemed to have disposed of your assets and investments for tax purposes in the year that you leave. RRIFs and RRSPs are an exception. You are under no obligation to withdraw your money from these vehicles, and in most cases, you are better off leaving it in because you are likely to pay more tax if you withdraw all of it. To the extent you make withdrawals out of these plans after you have left Canada, the Income Tax Act imposes a non-resident withholding tax that ranges from 0 percent to 25 percent depending on the amount and the country of emigration.

Note that the withholding tax might be reduced or waived in some jurisdictions if the amounts being withdrawn qualify as "periodic pension payments." For withdrawals from a RRIF, the amount is considered a periodic pension payment if the annual amount withdrawn does not exceed the minimum required withdrawal or, if greater, 10 percent of the fair market value of the RRIF at the beginning of the year.

Analysis of RRIF Rules

For many retirees, the knee-jerk reaction is to try to minimize the amount of income tax they pay from their retirement savings. This can lead to keeping the money in an RRSP until the age of 71 and then making the minimum withdrawals from that point on. You will note that this practice is precisely the opposite of what I am recommending in this book, especially with Enhancement 2. It involves deferring CPP pension until age 70 and drawing down your RRIF instead. By doing so, you are indeed paying more income tax from the RRIF but not more income tax overall. And in the long run, you will receive more total income by deferring CPP.

Life Income Funds (LIFs)

If your retirement savings came from a pension plan rather than an RRSP, you might transfer the account balance to a locked-in retirement account (LIRA) or a locked-in RRSP, where it would remain tax-sheltered until you are ready to start receiving payouts or until age 71, if earlier. When that time comes, the monies would be transferred to a LIF or the equivalent vehicle.

A LIF serves the same purpose as a RRIF. Both are vehicles from which you can receive regular income with the savings you accumulated. One fundamental difference is that LIF withdrawals are subject to a maximum percentage of assets (except in Saskatchewan). This means that the amount you can take out in a given year may be capped. All LIFs and equivalent vehicles are subject to the same minimum annual withdrawal as RRIFs, stated as a percentage of total assets as specified in Table B.1.

Equivalent Vehicles

LIF rules differ from province to province because the assets come from registered pension plans, which are subject to provincial pension legislation.* These variations by jurisdiction can make LIFs or their equivalent seem much more complicated. The best thing to do is to locate the rules below that pertain to your situation and filter out the rest.

In Newfoundland & Labrador, retirees also have the option of transferring their money to a locked-in retirement income fund (LRIF). Saskatchewan replaced LIFs with prescribed retirement income funds (PRIFs). LIFs still exist in the case of federally regulated organizations but have been displaced by restricted life income funds (RLIFs) to some extent. LRIFs, PRIFs, and RLIFs are all similar to LIFs except as indicated below.

Duration of a LIF

At one time in Newfoundland & Labrador and Saskatchewan, remaining LIF funds had to be used to purchase a life annuity at age 80. With the new vehicles (LRIFs and PRIFs respectively), this is no longer a requirement. Prince Edward Island has no LIF at all because it never enacted pension legislation. As a result, an RRIF is the only option available there. In all other provinces, a LIF normally continues for life unless the LIF holder withdraws the entire balance in cash when permissible or uses it to buy an annuity. Annuities purchased with LIFs might differ from annuities purchased with funds from RRIFs because certain spousal survivor benefits need to be included in the case of a LIF (unless the spouse waived them).

---

* Except in the case of federally regulated companies, which are subject to federal regulation that is very similar.

Cash-Out Options

Most jurisdictions allow LIF holders to transfer a portion of the LIF to a regular RRSP or a RRIF. If you want to pursue the decumulation strategy in this book, this option can be very important. Otherwise, the LIF maximum withdrawal rules in most jurisdictions make it more difficult to put Enhancement 2 into effect.

In Ontario, the LIF holder has the one-time option of transferring up to 50 percent of the LIF assets into a regular RRSP or a RRIF. The election must be within 60 days of transferring locked-in funds from a LIRA or a registered pension plan into the LIF. Alberta also gives the option to transfer up to 50 percent of locked-in assets to an RRSP or a RRIF, provided the LIF holder does so before transferring the rest of the assets to a LIF.

Before age 65, Quebecers can withdraw an additional amount from their LIFs equal to 40 percent of the Quebec pensionable earnings ceiling in that year. This supplement tides them over until government pensions start. Unfortunately, they do not have this option between the ages of 65 and 70, when it could be helpful in carrying out Enhancement 2.

In New Brunswick, the LIF owner has the one-time option to transfer LIF assets to a RRIF. The maximum transfer is three times the maximum withdrawal in that year or 25 percent of the LIF balance at the start of the year, whichever is less.

Manitoba LIF holders can make a one-time transfer to a PRIF of up to 50 percent of the value of their LIF. There are no restrictions within the PRIF as to how much can be withdrawn in a given year. In Saskatchewan, the PRIF has replaced the LIF. That makes Saskatchewan the only province with no restrictions on the amount that can be withdrawn in a given year.

If you worked for a federally regulated employer (for example, in transportation, banking, or communications), you can transfer your LIF assets to an RLIF. This is like a LIF except you have the one-time opportunity to transfer 50 percent of the assets to a regular RRSP or RRIF. This option must be elected within 60 days of opening the RLIF.

Maximum Annual Payouts

Payouts under a LIF are subject to a maximum, except in Saskatchewan. The maximum in any given year is calculated by dividing the LIF balance by an **annuity certain** factor. The term of the annuity is the number of years until the age of 90. The interest rate for the annuity is based on the CANSIM (Canadian socioeconomic database from Statistics Canada) interest rate from the preceding November or 6 percent, if greater. There are slight variations in some jurisdictions, as described below.

> An **annuity certain** is a stream of payments (usually equal) that is made for a fixed period, such as ten years. It differs from a life annuity, which is payable until death. The payments are based on a certain interest rate; the higher the rate, the higher the payments.

This is probably more information than you need to know. What is worth knowing is that the maximum withdrawal percentages will probably not change for many years to come. With interest rates so low, the 6 percent default rate underlying the annuity certain will be the applicable rate for the foreseeable future. The federal jurisdiction is the exception, as the 6 percent default rate does not apply. As a result, their maximum percentages are significantly lower (this includes PEI, which has no pension legislation of its own). Finally, the basis for the calculation is a little different in Quebec, Manitoba, and Nova Scotia.

Table B.3 shows the maximum percentage of assets that can be paid out of a LIF for each year from age 55 and on. For example, someone at age 58 in Manitoba can withdraw no more than 6.6 percent of her LIF assets in that year. Note that some provinces allow LIF payments before 55, but this is not shown here.

Table B.3. Maximum withdrawal percentages from a LIF

Age	Quebec, Manitoba, and Nova Scotia	All other provinces*
55	6.40%	6.51%
56	6.50%	6.57%
57	6.50%	6.63%
58	6.60%	6.70%
59	6.70%	6.77%
60	6.70%	6.85%
61	6.80%	6.94%
62	6.90%	7.04%
63	7.00%	7.14%
64	7.10%	7.26%
65	7.20%	7.38%
66	7.30%	7.52%
67	7.40%	7.67%
68	7.60%	7.83%
69	7.70%	8.02%
70	7.90%	8.22%
71	8.10%	8.45%
72	8.30%	8.71%
73	8.50%	9.00%
74	8.80%	9.34%
75	9.10%	9.71%
76	9.40%	10.15%
77	9.80%	10.66%
78	10.20%	11.25%
79	10.80%	11.96%
80	11.50%	12.82%
81	12.10%	13.87%
82	12.90%	15.19%
83	13.80%	16.90%
84	14.80%	19.19%

85	16.00%	22.40%
86	17.30%	27.23%
87	18.90%	35.29%
88	20.00%	51.46%
89	20.00%	100.00%
90+	20.00%	100.00%

*Except for federal jurisdiction, Newfoundland & Labrador, and the province of PEI, where the maximum is much lower. Also, the table does not reflect the modification to the maximum due to the previous year's investment return.

In British Columbia, Alberta, Manitoba, and Ontario, the maximum payment is the investment return in the previous year if that amount is greater than the percentage given in Table B.3. In Newfoundland & Labrador, the maximum payment on an LRIF is the investment return from the previous year. This means that the maximum will equal the minimum in most years, especially after age 70.

Analysis of LIFs

It is ironic that the maximum withdrawal rules do exactly the opposite of what they are intended to do. They are meant to enhance retirement security by ensuring that retirees don't outlive their assets. Unfortunately, the maximums make it more difficult to implement Enhancement 2. Fortunately, most retirees can get around this restriction by using the LIF cash-out option that is available in most jurisdictions coupled with the use of other assets such as TFSAs, RRSPs, and non-registered assets to generate income until they start CPP payments at age 70.

APPENDIX C

Details on Using PERC

As described in Chapter 15, Enhancement 4 involves using an online cal-culator to figure out how much income you can draw. While there is an online help feature (click on the "?"), explanations are kept intentionally short. This appendix provides more insight into how to complete the entries. I will also explain some of the implicit assumptions underlying the calculations.

The first question you are asked is if you are completing PERC for yourself only or whether you are including your spouse. In most cases, I strongly recommend including your spouse, since you are in it together and will be using the assets of both parties to provide joint income.

Table C.1 provides commentary on many of the questions asked by PERC. I will not comment on every question as some of them are quite straightforward.

Table C.1. How to complete the entries in PERC

Question	Comments
Your current age?	Note that you and your spouse need to be at least 50. This is a tool for immediate and soon-to-be retirees.
Gender?	This is needed to calculate annuity factors.
Monthly amount of your current CPP pension?	If you are not receiving CPP yet, this should be left blank. Do not enter 0.
Expected future CPP pension (as a %)?	You complete this only if you left the previous question blank. You might not know what your CPP pension will be but estimate it as closely as you can. If you always worked and always contributed more than the year's maximum pensionable earnings, your CPP pension should be 100%. Do not enter a figure higher than 100% because you deferred CPP until 70.
Monthly amount of your OAS pension?	Leave it blank if you are not receiving OAS yet.
Number of years you will have lived in Canada from ages 18 to 65?	The answer is used to estimate your OAS pension. If you have 40 years in Canada after 18, you will get the maximum OAS. PERC will calculate whether any of it is clawed back.
Amount in TFSA?	Enter the most recent balance.
Investable assets that are not tax-sheltered (NTS assets)?	This could be a bank account or stocks with a broker. Do not include real estate here.
Income tax rate you will pay on NTS assets when you sell?	If it is cash, then tax will already be paid. You should answer 0%. If it is a stock with a big capital gain, you will pay tax on half that gain. If the stock was up 20% since you bought it, you will pay about 4% or 5% in income tax.
Future "windfall," net of tax and expenses?	For instance, you might come into an inheritance someday or you might plan to downsize your home. If no windfall is expected, leave this blank.

Number of years before you will receive the windfall?	You might not know for certain, but try to estimate it as best you can. If more than ten years, then ignore the windfall.
Monthly rent or income you are getting from your investment property, net of expenses?	Note this is net of expenses and property tax. It is also net of mortgage payments you are making on that property.
The monthly amount of DB pension?	Complete this only if you participated in a DB pension plan at some point. This does not include CPP or OAS.
Future increases in DB pension (as a % of CPI)?	In some plans, the increases are automatic. In other plans, the employer decides whether to grant increases. Make your best estimate of the average increase.
Annual amount of prescribed annuity you have?	A prescribed annuity is something you buy with after-tax dollars, not with your RRSP. If it is paid monthly, convert to annual by multiplying by 12.
Amount of debt you still expect to have next year?	This debt could be a mortgage on your home or a line of credit.
Are you self-employed?	This is important because you have to contribute double the usual amount toward CPP.
Amount that you plan to contribute annually to an RRSP?	This is important for users who still have a few working years left. It enables them to add to their RRSP.

Once you have completed all the entries, PERC will show you results under three scenarios:

- Scenario 1 — Poor investment returns, results before the enhancements
- Scenario 2 — Poor returns, results after the enhancements
- Scenario 3 — Median investment returns, results after the enhancements

The purpose of Scenario 1 is to establish a base and thus show how much the enhancements can improve your retirement situation. I believe you should always be drawing income that is between Scenarios 2 and 3, assuming you adopt the enhancements. You should rerun PERC annually because these amounts will change as your circumstances change.

Besides showing the gross amount of income you can draw under each scenario, PERC also estimates how much you can *spend*. This is a different figure since it takes into account the approximate income tax you will pay and the OAS clawback. Before retirement, it is offset by payments toward debt and contributions to RRSPs and TFSAs.

Table C.2 gives a description of the principal assumptions used in the calculations.

Table C.2. Assumptions used in the calculations in PERC

Income-drawing strategy	It is assumed that no more than 10% of the tax-sheltered assets are drawn in each of the early years. Also, 10% of the TFSA assets are drawn each year. The balance is drawn from NTS assets. This approach smooths out the tax impact over time.
Tax calculation	Couples are assumed to make full use of income-splitting after 65 and to use all tax credits.
Future adjustments to income	Total income is assumed to rise in accordance with the spending rate described in Chapter 5. The long-term inflation rate is assumed to be 2.2% a year.
Assets remaining	In calculating the income targets, it is assumed that an amount equal to 10% of the initial assets must remain at age 95 under the worst-case scenario and age 92 under the median-return scenario.
Asset mix in the RRIF and TFSA	30% in Canadian stocks (S&P/TSX Capped Composite Index), 30% in foreign stocks (MSCI World Index), and 40% in Canadian government bonds (FTSE TMX Canada Universe Bond Index).

Enhancements	In Scenarios 2 and 3, it is assumed that Enhancements 1, 2, and 3 are adopted unless this is not possible (e.g., the user is already drawing CPP). Enhancement 2 is taken to mean deferral of CPP to 70, although 70 is not always the optimal age.
Investment fees	Investment fees are assumed to be 1.80% a year under Scenario 1 and 0.6% a year under Scenarios 2 and 3.
OAS clawback	It is assumed the clawback will rise annually with inflation.
Interest rate for annuity purchase	2.50%
Type of annuity	Joint and two-thirds survivor annuity for couples, life-only annuity with five-year guarantee for single retirees.
Future investment returns	For safe income target, 5th-percentile returns based on a Monte Carlo simulation. For best-estimate scenario, median returns from the same simulation.
Allowance for spending shocks	Shocks are assumed to be absorbed by a reserve fund set up in retirement by saving 3% of annual income until age 75.

Limitations

PERC should be useful but it is far from perfect. Here are some of the key limitations to PERC:

1. A user with multiple sources of income cannot vary which source is used first to produce income. (See "Income-drawing strategy" in the above table.)
2. The tax calculations are based on the Ontario tax tables; the tables for other provinces will vary somewhat.
3. Projections are based only on a 60-40 asset mix, which will not suit every retiree.

4. The underlying interest rate for annuity purchases is 2.5 percent. Historically this has been very conservative, but that is not the case at the present time.

5. The user might want to put aside 4 or 5 percent to create a reserve for spending shocks; also, you might want to continue contributing to this reserve until age 80, instead of stopping at 75. PERC does not allow these variations.

6. The amount of assets you wish to have remaining at the end of life (which is assumed to be in your 90s) is assumed to be 10 percent of the initial tax-sheltered assets. If you wish to retain more, you will have to understate your initial assets.

As mentioned, the PERC calculator can be found at perc.morneau shepell.com. There is no charge for using it.

Disclaimers

Here are a few important disclaimers:

1. Use PERC at your own risk. It is impossible to reflect all possible scenarios.

2. These results are only as good as the data used to create the Monte Carlo simulations. The underlying assumptions will never be perfect.

3. The income tax calculations are only an approximation, based on the current income tax rates in Ontario. No attempt is made to calculate the impact of tax loss carryforwards. For future years, all tax credits and income tax brackets are assumed to rise with general inflation.

4. The risk of much higher inflation is not reflected since an aging population makes it highly unlikely for many years to come.

5. While the intention is to maintain PERC indefinitely, the author and Morneau Shepell reserve the right to discontinue it or to stop maintaining it at any time.

APPENDIX D

Quirky CPP Rules You Should Know About

The Canada Pension Plan contains some peculiar rules that seem to defy logic and are certainly not what the average enlightened layperson would expect. In fact, they do not even make sense to many pension experts. The pension plans maintained by the federal government for civil servants do not have similar rules, even though it is those civil servants who dreamt up the rules for the CPP. It is important to know about these anomalies because they might affect your retirement planning.

Survivor Pension

It is a fair guess that fewer than a dozen people in Canada can explain how the survivor pensions under the CPP are calculated. And I am not even talking about the fact that the rules are different depending on whether the surviving spouse is over or under age 65. Let's restrict our focus only to the situation where the surviving spouse is 65 or over. Let's assume that Nick is 68 at the time of death and Susan is 65. Nick's basic retirement pension (BRP-Nick) is $14,000 a year based on retirement at

65. Susan's basic retirement pension (BRP-Susan) is $9,800 a year if she starts CPP at 65.

The basic rule is that the surviving spouse pension is 60 percent of the deceased spouse's basic retirement pension. Which means that Susan should receive 60 percent of Nick's $14,000 BRP, or $8,400. If only it were that simple!

The first complication is that the survivor benefit is capped. Susan's basic CPP retirement pension plus the survivor benefit cannot exceed the maximum CPP payable to one person. In this case, the sum of the two would be $18,200, which is nearly $4,000 more than the maximum. To calculate Susan's actual survivor benefit, you need to determine A, B, and C:

$$A = 60\% \text{ of BRP-Nick} - 40\% \text{ of } 60\% \text{ of BRP-Nick} = \$5{,}040$$
$$B = 60\% \text{ of BRP-Nick} - 40\% \text{ of BRP-Susan} = \$4{,}480$$

You take the lesser of A and B, which is $4,480. You then compare this number to C where:

$$C = \text{BRP-Nick} - \text{BRP-Susan} = \$4{,}200$$

Since C is lower, that is Susan's survivor benefit.

The other quirk is that the survivor benefit is not based on the CPP pension the deceased spouse was actually receiving, but on what they would have been receiving had they started to take CPP at 65. For instance, if Nick had deferred his CPP pension to age 68 so he was receiving $17,360 a year instead of $14,000, you would think the above survivor benefit calculations would use the higher number. They don't, however.

By the way, if Susan had deferred her CPP pension to age 70, she would not be receiving any basic retirement pension when Nick died. As a result, calculation C above would not apply (at least not until Susan is 70) and calculation B would be modified to 60 percent of Nick's basic retirement pension (60 percent of $14,000). The resulting survivor benefit is $8,400, though it would reduce to $4,200 when Susan turned 70 and started her own basic CPP pension. This gives her an added incentive to wait until 70 to start her own CPP.

Requirement to Contribute after Age 65

In Chapter 11, I showed that it usually makes sense (financially) to start your CPP pension at age 70 instead of 65. If you continue to earn employment income after 65, though, you might have second thoughts about this strategy.

Consider a pair of twins, Borden and Hart. Both of them worked from age 23 to age 65 and both earned enough each year to contribute the maximum to the CPP. As a result, they both qualify for the maximum CPP pension at age 65, which we will assume is $1,200 a month.

Hart (who is self-employed) defers the start of his CPP pension and continues to work until 70. (In fact, he'll probably work until 85, but that's another story.) As a result, he is forced to contribute about $6,000 a year for the next five years. (We will ignore increases in the CPP earnings ceiling.) By age 70, he will have contributed about another $30,000. The CPP pension he gets at age 70 (ignoring inflation again) is $1,704 a month.

Borden also defers the start of his CPP pension. The difference is that he stops working at 65. He makes no further contributions to the CPP between 65 and 70. At age 70, his CPP pension is $1,704 a month, the same as it is for Hart. To be clear, Hart contributed about $30,000 more over a five-year period and gets nothing for it.*

Forcing Hart to contribute is blatantly unfair. It is so unfair that even some of the staff at the federal department where they administer CPP benefits use their common sense rather than following the rules. As a result, they get it wrong sometimes and take people like Hart off the hook.

Forced contributions after 65 are especially unfair because the federal government's pension plan for civil servants, the Public Service Pension Plan, doesn't even allow (much less require) employees to keep on contributing after 35 years of making contributions.** If the government really wants to encourage people to keep working *and* implement an effective decumulation strategy, they should rethink the rules about

---

* I'm ignoring a tiny sliver of extra CPP pension that Hart gets due to the new CPP rules being phased in.

** Apart from a piddling 1 percent of pay for automatic inflation protection.

contributing after 65. The current rules have the effect of neutralizing the beneficial effect of Enhancement 2 or discouraging people from working past 65.

ACKNOWLEDGEMENTS

The book would never have been written if I didn't happen to attend a presentation in the summer of 2016 given by two highly respected Morneau Shepell actuaries — Nigel Branker and Emily Tryssenaar. They alerted me to the fact that maximizing income from savings while minimizing risk was far from simple.

At the time I wrote the first edition in 2017, I was still employed by Morneau Shepell. The firm provided me with considerable support and encouragement, and in particular I am grateful to Stephen Liptrap, president and CEO of Morneau Shepell, who freed up my time and gave me the resources I needed to write the book. The Morneau Shepell Retirement Solutions practice ran the Monte Carlo simulations that underlie much of the hard analysis contained in the book.

Michelle Massie, my wife, kindly put up with me during the many months when I was preoccupied with the writing of the book and again when I revised it to produce this second edition.

My investment advisor, Franco Barbiero of RBC Wealth Management, has been supportive in many ways, including offering me RBC's research capabilities as well as his home laptop when I forgot mine in California!

Tess Francis of CIBC Financial Planning provided me with a great deal of useful information to improve on the RRIF summary that I had in the first edition.

Malcolm Hamilton, Canada's pension guru for the past 30 years, was generous with his time in helping to frame the basic arguments and acting as a sounding board in the early stages of the writing process.

Ed Caffyn used the skills that he cultivated over a brilliant career in advertising to provide many ideas for the redesign of the cover of the book. ECW Press was responsible for the final cover design and did an admirable job.

Bonnie-Jeanne MacDonald, director of financial security research at Ryerson University's National Institute on Ageing, was helpful in identifying relevant academic papers and providing feedback in other ways.

Christopher Cottier, an investment adviser in Vancouver also known as "Eagle Eyes," provided a very useful technical edit of the book. Other people who provided input were sons Troy and Gregory, Toronto financial planner Rona Birenbaum, and my good friend and former colleague Michele Kumara.

Finally, I want to thank the team at ECW Press, Jennifer Smith in particular, for taking me under their wing and making this second edition happen.

ENDNOTES

Chapter 5

1. *Society of Actuaries 2015 Risks and Process of Retirement Survey: Report of Findings.* A US survey conducted on behalf of the society by Mathew Greenwald & Associates, Inc.
2. Stephen P. Bonnar, "Consumption Patterns of the Elderly" (master's thesis, McMaster University, 2016), 82.
3. Geoffrey N. Calvert, *Pensions and Survival: The Coming Crisis of Money and Retirement* (Toronto: Maclean-Hunter, 1977).
4. Benjamin Tal, "The Looming Bequest Boom — What Should We Expect?" *In Focus* newsletter. CIBC. June 2016.
5. Axel Börsch-Supan, "Savings and Consumption Patterns of the Elderly — The German Case," *Journal of Population Economics* 5 (1992).
6. Malcolm Hamilton, "The Financial Circumstances of Elderly Canadians and the Implications for the Design of Canada's Retirement Income System," in *The State of Economics in Canada* (Montreal: McGill-Queen's University Press, 2001).

7. David Domeij and Magnus Johannesson, "Consumption and Health," *The B.E. Journal of Macroeconomics* 6, no. 1 (2006).

8. Cesira Urzi Brancati, Brian Beach, Ben Franklin, and Matthew Jones, *Understanding Retirement Journeys — Expectations vs Reality.* International Longevity Centre UK. November 2015.

9. McKinsey & Company, *Building on Canada's Strong Retirement Readiness.* February 2015.

10. Catherine Michaud, "Development of a Consumer Price Index for Seniors," Statistics Canada. June 2019.

Chapter 6

1. *Society of Actuaries 2015 Risks and Process of Retirement Survey: Report of Findings,* 125.

Chapter 10

1. Robert D. Arnott, Jason Hsu, and Vitali Kalesnik, "The Surprising Alpha from Malkiel's Monkey and Upside-Down Strategies," *Practical Applications* 1, no. 2 (2013).

Chapter 26

1. Steve Vernon, *The Next Evolution in Defined Contribution Retirement Plan Design.* Leland Stanford Junior University. September 2013.

2. Association of Canadian Pension Management. *Decumulation, The Next Critical Frontier: Improvements for Defined Contribution and Capital Accumulation Plans.* March 2017.

INDEX

Note: Page numbers in bold indicate a chart or a table.

Association of Canadian Pension Management (ACPM), 166

backstop (Enhancement 5). *See* home equity line of credit (HELOC) (Enhancement 5); reverse mortgage (Enhancement 5)
basis point, 10, 11, 70
bear markets, 58–59, 60, 183, 190n
benchmarks, 70–72, **71**
bequests, 156–60; about, 156; accidental, 156–57, 160, 186; altruistic, 157; changing circumstances, 159; downside of, 160, 187; home equity, 158–59, 160, 186–87; and inheritances, 159–60; by mainstream retirees, 7, 124, 156–57, 158; making vs not making, 157–58; RRIF, 193; strategic, 157
bird in the hand argument, 81
black swans, 54–60; about, 54–55; bear markets, 58–59, 60, 183; COVID-19 pandemic, 55–57; defined, 54–55; vs other scenarios, 60; survival strategies, 59–60
Blanchett, David, 28
bonds: alternatives, 48–49; and annuities, 93–94; COVID-19 pandemic, 57; future returns, 44, 53; high yield, 48; long term, 49–50, 53, 169, 183; real return bonds, 49–50, 53; vs stocks, 45, 48, 49, 50, 51
Borden and Hart (case study), 208
Börsch-Supan, Axel, 26, 27
Brancati study, 27, 28–29
Browning, Kurt, 109

Calvert, Geoffrey, 24
Canada Pension Plan Investment Board (CPPIB), 83
Canadian Institute of Actuaries (CIA), 70, 166
CANSIM (Canadian socioeconomic database from Statistics Canada), 197
capital gains, 44, 47, 94, 139, 148–49
case studies' asset mix, 52
checklist for enhancements, 63–64, 183
children, grown, 64; annuities, 95; bequests, 157–58, 159, 160, 187; inheritance, 125; spending shocks, 14, 16, 19–20, 22, 182
Clarkes (case study), 143–46; adopt enhancements, 144–46; before enhancements, **145**; financial overview, 143–44, **144**
Cleaver, Beaver, 125–26
Cleavers, the (as type), 125–26, 157
corporate image, and pension plans, 176–77, 179, 188
corroboration, of decumulation strategies, 165–66
COVID-19 pandemic (2020), 55–57, 59, 93
CPP: applying for, 81–82; calculation of, 76–77; compared to Social Security, 84; contribution requirements, 208–9; defined, 10; dilution, 130, 132, 186; early retirement vs delaying, 76–77; maximum amount, 75, 75n; at retirement, 9; stability of, 83–84, 108, 154; survivor pension, 120, 123, 206–7; and working past 65, 86. *See also* CPP deferral

FREDERICK VETTESE is Canada's most visible actuary. His entire career has been focused on working within Canada's retirement income system. For 27 years, he was chief actuary of Morneau Shepell, a Canadian HR services firm with 6,000 employees and 24,000 clients. Frederick now spends most of his professional time speaking and writing about retirement issues. He has written over 100 articles and op-eds for the *Globe and Mail* and the *National Post* alone. He also has two other retirement books to his credit. Fred can be reached through LinkedIn.